IMAGES of America

MISSOURI IN WORLD WAR I

ON THE COVER: Soldiers of Company H, 6th Missouri Infantry, a Missouri National Guard company located in Dexter, are pictured at Camp Clark near Nevada, Missouri, prior to movement to Camp Doniphan, Oklahoma, to prepare for World War I. The 3rd Missouri Infantry and 6th Missouri Infantry merged during the war to form the 140th Infantry Regiment. (Author's collection.)

IMAGES
of America

MISSOURI IN WORLD WAR I

Jeremy Paul Amick

ARCADIA
PUBLISHING

ISBN 978-1-4671-0513-2

Published by Arcadia Publishing
Charleston, South Carolina

Printed in the United States of America

Library of Congress Control Number: 2019955539

For all general information, please contact Arcadia Publishing:
Telephone 843-853-2070
Fax 843-853-0044
E-mail sales@arcadiapublishing.com
For customer service and orders:
Toll-Free 1-888-313-2665

Visit us on the Internet at www.arcadiapublishing.com

This work is dedicated to the 156,000 Missourians who served in all branches of the US armed forces during World War I, and the more than 10,000 of our state's heroes who surrendered their lives in the cause for freedom.

Contents

Acknowledgments

The majority of the photographs in this compilation come from the personal collection of the author, but there are additional contributors who helped ensure this work arrived at a successful conclusion. First, I wish to thank my friend Charles Machon, director of the Museum of Missouri Military History, for his contributions to this endeavor. Additionally, I extend my gratitude to the Missouri State Museum/Missouri State Parks for granting access to several of their photographs. As always, thank you for your assistance in helping preserve our state's military legacy.

Introduction

It is truly challenging to detail the story of World War I without mention of the significant contributions made by Missouri in the war effort. When tens of thousands of doughboys deployed overseas to fight for the cause of freedom, their commander, Gen. John J. Pershing, was a native of the state, having been born and raised in the vicinity of Laclede. Approximately 30 miles to the north in Grundy County, another Missourian with a successful career in the US Army, Enoch Crowder, attained the esteemed rank of major general and became the primary author of the Selective Service Act of 1917—the military draft instrument that helped build the military force that valiantly fought under General Pershing overseas. The state also demonstrated its abilities in aerial warfare by producing two celebrated flying aces. Additionally, the US Navy became a beneficiary of Missouri-born leadership with notables such as Admirals Robert E. Coontz and Arthur Willard.

World War I was a period of great change for the Missouri National Guard. Prior to the country's entry into the war, the National Defense Act of 1916 was enacted as a means to integrate the National Guard as an element of the US Army. On August 5, 1917, approximately four months after the United States officially declared war against Germany, Pres. Woodrow Wilson drafted the entire National Guard into federal service. During the war, the regiments of the Missouri National Guard were consolidated, many becoming machine-gun battalions. William Robertson, who served in the US Army Air Service during the war, later became an aviation pioneer in the Missouri National Guard and helped in the establishment of Lambert Field, which has since grown into St. Louis Lambert International Airport.

The legacy of the Show-Me State in the "Great War" is also revealed through the efforts of the American Red Cross. During the war, scores of volunteers joined the organization and not only provided critical medical support through overseas hospitals, but assisted on the home front in communities such as St. Louis during the Spanish influenza pandemic. The Salvation Army also rose to the occasion and embraced the volunteer spirit of a number of women from throughout the state, many of whom were sent overseas to help fry donuts and serve coffee to combat-weary troops.

Camp Clark, near Nevada, Missouri, became a marshalling site for federalized Missouri National Guard troops while Jefferson Barracks served as a major mobilization site for the US Army. The three military academies in the state at the time—Kemper Military School in Boonville, Wentworth Military Academy in Lexington, and Missouri Military Academy in Mexico—worked with the War Department to ensure their cadets received adequate training to serve as leaders in the military. In Kansas City, Sweeney Automotive and Tractor School, in addition to Rahe's Auto and Tractor School, tailored its curriculum to prepare mechanics who would go on to serve during the war. The employees of the St. Charles Car Company, which manufactured passenger railcars, joined the war effort by producing components for artillery pieces, while ranches and farms throughout the state raised thousands of mules that hauled supplies and equipment in France.

Missouri also played a unique role in the formation of the American Legion. In March 1919 during the Paris Caucus, where hundreds of American servicemembers met while still overseas to discuss forming an organization comprised of veterans who served in the war, Col. Bennett Champ Clark, a veteran from Bowling Green, was elected first national commander of the American Legion. From May 8 to May 10, 1919, the St. Louis Caucus was held as a follow-up to the initial caucus in Paris and resulted in the approval of drafts of the organization's preamble and constitution. Three years later, the American Legion held its third national convention in Kansas City, which was attended by the five Allied military leaders of World War I, including General Pershing. It was during this event that the site for the Liberty Memorial was dedicated, an impressive edifice now situated on the site of the National World War I Museum and Memorial. When American Legion posts began to spring up throughout Missouri after the war, tributes for the sacrifices of many state residents who lost their lives in the conflict were made in the naming of the posts in their honor.

In the years following the armistice, many forms of memorials and monuments were erected to honor both those who served and those who never made it home from the war. One of the most profound is Memorial Tower at the University of Missouri in Columbia. This grand structure has seen additions since its initial opening in 1926; however, it remains a testament to the 117 university students who lost their lives to disease or in combat during the war. In other communities such as Kansas City, the Daughters of the American Revolution commissioned a beautiful painting called *The Call of Missouri* to commemorate those from the state who served in World War I. Sadly, the painting later disappeared and was sold at auction to an unknown private collector several years ago.

Missouri in World War I is by no means an all-inclusive chronicle with regard to the critical role the state played during this influential worldwide conflict, yet it highlights many of the important contributions made by the state's citizens. My hope it that it inspires a greater admiration for the rich history of our state and a renewed appreciation of the sacrifices made by countless service members on the battlefields of France.

One

A State of Influence

Missouri native Gen. John J. Pershing visits in the Governor's Garden in Paris with French military commander Joseph Joffre. Early in World War I, Joffre became a national hero to the French people for his victory at the First Battle of the Marne in 1914. Joffre remained commander in chief of the French forces until his resignation in 1916, at which time he was replaced by Robert Nivelle.

General Pershing, right, is pictured in this US Army Signal Corps photograph from June 1918 visiting in Chaumont, France, with Marshal Ferdinand Foch, a French general and supreme Allied commander during the latter part of World War I. Initially, Pershing was opposed to amalgamation—the insertion of American troops directly into French and British units. Instead, Pershing allowed for the amalgamation of American forces at the division level. This arrangement resulted in American soldiers taking their orders from American officers up to the level of major general but with strategic direction from more experienced French officers at the corps, army, and army group levels.

General Pershing is pictured with his son Francis Warren shortly after the end of World War I. In 1915, while Pershing was commanding troops during the Punitive Expedition in Mexico, his wife and three young daughters perished from smoke inhalation in a fire at their home at the Presidio in San Francisco. Francis Warren was the only child of Pershing to survive the tragedy, and he later achieved the rank of colonel, serving as an advisor to George C. Marshall in World War II.

A native of Grundy County, Missouri, Enoch Herbert Crowder graduated from West Point in 1881. During his four years at the academy, he did not distinguish himself among his peers when it came to academics, ranking 31st in a class of 54. In later years, he emerged from his shell, rising to the rank of major general and achieving recognition as one of the greatest judge advocate generals of the US Army. Crowder is pictured in his West Point graduation photograph from 1881.

During World War I, Maj. Gen. Enoch Crowder became the principal author of the Selective Service Act of 1917, which established the parameters of drafting into military service the scores of troops who would go on to achieve victory in Europe with the American Expeditionary Forces under the command of fellow Missourian and US Army general John J. Pershing.

Frederick D. Gardner, pictured, served as governor of Missouri during the period of World War I, from 1917 to 1921. On April 12, 1917, at the request of Secretary of War Newton D. Baker, Governor Gardner established the Missouri Council of Defense and appointed as chairman Frederick B. Mumford, the dean of the Missouri College of Agriculture. The council served as the coordinating body between federal government and state departments, encouraging patriotism while also coordinating the state's resources for various programs in support of the war effort. Initially, the council's focus was on increased farm production and reducing food consumption.

Maj. Gen. Leonard Wood is a name that has been associated with Missouri since Fort Leonard Wood came into existence during the Second World War. A native of New Hampshire, Wood was awarded the Medal of Honor for his role during the Apache Wars years earlier. In World War I, he was engaged in noncombat roles of training for the 10th and 89th Divisions at Camp Funston, Kansas.

Adm. Robert E. Coontz was born and raised in Hannibal and graduated from the US Naval Academy in 1885. He distinguished himself during World War I as commandant of the Puget Sound Naval Yard and the 13th Naval District. During his impressive and lengthy military career, he achieved the rank of four-star admiral and was selected to serve as chief of naval operations in 1919. The veteran passed away in 1935 after suffering a series of heart attacks and was laid to rest in Mount Olivet Cemetery in Hannibal.

ADMIRAL R. E. COONTZ, CHIEF OF NAVAL OPERATIONS.

Adm. (Ret.) Robert E. Coontz, left, is pictured in May 1933 presenting an anchor made of buddy poppies to Claude E. Swanson, who was serving as secretary of the Navy. The anchor was made in honor of Memorial Day and cast upon the waters of the Potomac River in recognition of sailors of the US Navy who lost their lives in World War I. At the time of the presentation, Coontz was serving as commander in chief of the Veterans of Foreign Wars. (International News Photos/Author's collection.)

Vice Adm. Arthur Lee Willard, left, shakes hands with Adm. William Cole in 1930 after Willard relieved Cole as commander of the US Navy Scouting Fleet during ceremonies held aboard the USS *Wyoming* at the Brooklyn Navy Yard. Born in Kirksville in 1870, Willard graduated from the US Naval Academy in 1891. During World War I, the president awarded Willard a Navy Cross for his performance as superintendent of the Naval Gun Factory at the Washington Navy Yard. The Missouri native passed away in 1935 and was laid to rest in Arlington National Cemetery.

Omar Bradley, a native of Clark in Randolph County, graduated from West Point in 1915. His graduating class earned the nickname the "class the stars fell on" since 59 of the 164 graduates later attained the rank of general. During World War I, although Bradley was prepared to serve in France, he was sent to Butte, Montana, with the 14th Infantry Regiment to guard valuable copper mines from which the raw materials were extracted to produce casings for bullets and bombs.

Despite the importance of having guarded such a strategic resource during World War I, Lieutenant Bradley was frustrated that he had not been given the opportunity to join the scores of his fellow soldiers who fought overseas. During the Second World War, Gen. Omar Bradley would serve as a senior American commander and in 1950 was promoted to the rank of five-star general, serving as the first chairman of the Joint Chiefs of Staff.

George E. Creel was a native of Lafayette County and never finished his high school education. In the years prior to World War I, he was employed in the newspaper industry, fulfilling several roles such as reporter, editor, and publisher. During the war, he was asked by Pres. Woodrow Wilson to serve as chairman of the Committee on Public Information (CPI)—a temporary federal agency that embraced various forms of propaganda to solicit Americans' support for the war effort.

One initiative developed by the Committee on Public Information was known as the "4 Minute Men." They were groups of volunteers who were prepared to give four-minute speeches intended to inspire support for the war effort wherever they could find an audience—whether it be at restaurants, churches, movie theaters, or labor halls. This poster was developed by the CPI to advertise the program. (American Legion Post 5.)

Raised in Kansas City, Kate Richards O'Hare joined the Socialist Party of America in 1901 and became an organizer and supporter of labor unions. During World War I, she was vocal in her opposition to the country's involvement in the war and was sentenced to five years in prison for violations of the Espionage Act of 1917 and the Sedition Act of 1918, which made it illegal to interfere with the war effort. Following her early release from prison in 1920, O'Hare's lifelong mission became the reformation of the country's penal system.

Capt. Alexander Skinker, a native of St. Louis, was serving in France with Company I, 138th Infantry Regiment—a federalized Missouri National Guard company under the 35th Division—when he was killed in action on September 26, 1918, at Cheppy, France. On the date of his death, he led an attack on enemy machine-gun positions, seizing ammunition and feeding an automatic rifle until he was killed. His conspicuous gallantry earned him the Medal of Honor. The veteran is interred in Bellefontaine Cemetery in St. Louis.

Charles Denver Barger was born in Lawrence County in southwest Missouri in 1892. As a young boy, he was adopted by the Barger family after his father went to prison and his mother placed him in an orphanage. During World War I, he was drafted into the 89th Infantry Division and distinguished himself during the Meuse-Argonne Offensive when he and a fellow soldier went into enemy territory to rescue three wounded comrades. For his gallantry, Barger was presented with the Medal of Honor by a fellow Missourian, General Pershing.

John Barkley was serving at Cunel, France, during the Meuse-Argonne Offensive on October 7, 1918, when he successfully repaired a captured enemy machine gun, mounted it on a French tank, and twice repelled German counterattacks. This brave action earned him the Medal of Honor. In the years after the war, he was active in the creation of the Johnson County Park System, worked as a dairy farmer, and later became a land developer. He passed away on April 14, 1966, and is interred in Forest Hill Cemetery in Kansas City.

Michael B. Ellis, a native of St. Louis, was serving near Exermont, France, with Company C, 28th Infantry, 1st Division when on October 5, 1918, he voluntarily operated in front of his company, single-handedly attacking machine-gun nests and capturing numerous enemy soldiers. For his valor, he was awarded the Medal of Honor.

Born in Bolivar, M. Waldo Hatler was drafted into Company B, 356th Infantry Regiment in the spring of 1918. On November 8, 1918, while serving in France during World War I, Hatler was part of a patrol sent to recon the banks of the Meuse River. The means of crossing the river had been destroyed by the Germans, and Hatler and a fellow soldier volunteered to swim across to perform the recon. Hatler was the only one to survive the crossing and, after taking note of enemy positions, swam back across the river to provide his report. For his heroic actions, he was awarded the Medal of Honor.

Sgt. Arthur J. Forrest, a native of Hannibal, was serving with Company D, 354th Infantry Regiment of the 89th Division when he individually attacked an emplacement of six German machine guns that were halting the advance of his company on November 1, 1918. For his actions, he was awarded the Medal of Honor. The 69-year-old veteran died in St. Louis on November 30, 1964, and is interred in Grand View Burial Park in Hannibal.

Ernest Hemingway was working as a young reporter for the *Kansas City Star* when he made the decision to join the 7th Infantry Regiment of the Missouri National Guard in 1917. During his one year of service, he completed training with his company in the city's famed Swope Park. Although he was still too young to serve in the war without parental permission, Hemingway joined the Red Cross in 1918 and served with its ambulance corps in Italy. On the evening of July 8, 1918, he was wounded by an Austrian mortar shell and spent the remainder of the war recovering in a Red Cross hospital. Several of his wartime experiences reemerged in his writings, including the novel *A Farewell to Arms*.

Thomas Hart Benton was born in 1889 in the community of Neosho, and in later years studied art in Chicago and Paris. During World War I, he enlisted with the US Navy and was eventually transferred to the Intelligence Service, spending his wartime service drawing sketches of the naval base being constructed at Norfolk, Virginia. According to an article in the March 31, 1935, edition of the *St. Louis Post-Dispatch*, he spent the last seven months of his military service exhibiting these sketches in New York. (Museum of Missouri Military History.)

In the years following his World War I service, Thomas Hart Benton became a renowned artist who drew and painted scores of portraits, landscapes, and murals. He spent many years traveling, using the inspiration found in these journeys in the work he produced. In 1935, he moved to Kansas City, where he continued to reside until his death in 1975. A bronze bust of the World War I veteran and painter is featured in the Hall of Famous Missourians displayed in the Missouri State Capitol.

Bennett Champ Clark is pictured in 1930, shortly after announcing his intention of running for US senator for Missouri, an office he was elected to in 1932. During World War I, Clark was the youngest member of the American Expeditionary Forces to achieve the rank of colonel, serving overseas from April 25, 1918, to April 25, 1919, with the 140th Infantry Regiment, which had been formed under the 35th Division by the consolidation of two Missouri National Guard regiments.

Born in Bethany, Missouri, in 1901, Frank Buckles was the oldest living American military veteran of World War I when he passed away in 2011 at the advanced age of 110. He enlisted in the US Army in August 1917 when only 16 years old and spent most of the war in France driving motorcycles to deliver dispatches and shuttle officers, in addition to operating ambulances near the front lines. Following his passing, the Missouri native was laid to rest in Arlington National Cemetery. (Museum of Missouri Military History.)

Harvey Clark was a cadet at the former Wentworth Military Academy in Lexington and a veteran of the Spanish-American War. He became a brigadier general in 1899 and served as commander of the Laredo District during the Punitive Expedition to Mexico. During World War I, he was found medically unfit for overseas duty due to a tubercular condition but was appointed adjutant general of the Missouri National Guard in 1918 by Gov. Frederick Gardner. During and after World War I, Clark oversaw several state programs providing benefits and services to returning veterans. The 51-year-old Clark died in 1921. Camp Clark, near Nevada, was named in his honor. (Museum of Missouri Military History.)

Henry Robinson Clay Jr. of Plattsburg became one of two flying aces from Missouri during World War I. His aerial distinction came while assigned to the Royal Flying Corps as pilot of an iconic aircraft known as a Sopwith Camel—a British biplane. The 23-year-old died of pneumonia while stationed in Coblenz, Germany, shortly after the war's end.

Missouri's second flying ace of World War I was Oren Rose, a native of Bean Lake. Rose enlisted in the Canadian Royal Flying Corps and trained at a flight school in Texas. After arriving in England during the war, he distinguished himself as a combat aviator with 16 aerial victories.

During World War I, Oren Rose primarily piloted a Royal Aircraft S.E.5.—a British biplane. Although he was shot down on eight separate occasions, he returned from the war and went on to fly combat missions in the Russian Civil War in 1919 before becoming a flight instructor at a school in Los Angeles. The World War I flying ace passed away in 1971 and is buried in California.

Two

The Missouri National Guard

William A Raupp of Pierce City, Missouri, was for many years affiliated with the 2nd Missouri Infantry Regiment of the Missouri National Guard. He served during the Spanish-American War and later in the Punitive Expedition to Mexico. During World War I, after the 2nd Infantry was broken up into machine-gun companies, Colonel Raupp eventually became commander of the 60th Pioneer Infantry Regiment, which remained in Spartanburg, South Carolina, through the armistice. In 1921, he was appointed adjutant general of the Missouri National Guard following the death of Gen. Harvey C. Clark. Raupp died in 1946 and is buried in Pierce City Cemetery.

Gen. William Raupp, left, adjutant general of the Missouri National Guard, is pictured enjoying a break with some of his colonels during training exercises at Camp Clark, Missouri, a few years after the end of World War I. Located near Nevada, Missouri, Camp Clark became the assembly point for several Missouri National Guard regiments in World War I, most of which were federalized and broken up into machine-gun companies.

Col. Edward Moses Stayton of Independence had only recently returned from his command of Battery C, 1st Missouri Field Artillery in the Mexican Border Campaign when he was called into federal service in August 1917 to command the 110th Engineers of the Missouri National Guard in France. Retiring as a major general in 1938, Stayton served a term as commander for the state department of the American Legion in Missouri. A member of the Liberty Memorial Association, Stayton passed away in 1954 and is buried in Woodlawn Cemetery in Independence.

Col. Albert Linxwiler served several years in both the Illinois and Missouri National Guard and participated in three military engagements—the Spanish-American War, the Mexican Border Campaign, and World War I. He was commander of the newly formed 140th Infantry Regiment when it deployed overseas in World War I, but he left the regiment to serve in other leadership capacities to include "faithful and conscientious" duty during the Meuse-Argonne Offensive. Months after the armistice, he returned stateside with the regiment in May 1919.

This collar disk from Company H, 2nd Missouri Infantry was worn by Missouri National Guardsmen in the years prior to World War I. Located in Lebanon, Missouri, Company H mobilized in June 1916 and served during the Mexican Border Campaign. On August 5, 1917, the entire 2nd Missouri Infantry Regiment was again mobilized into federal service, and Company H became Company C, 129th Machine Gun Battalion for service overseas during World War I.

Missouri National Guard soldiers assigned to Company M, 2nd Missouri Infantry Regiment wore collar disks similar to this on their uniforms prior to World War I. When the 2nd Missouri was mobilized for World War I on August 5, 1917, it assembled at Camp Clark before moving to Camp Doniphan at Fort Sill, Oklahoma, for further training. While in Oklahoma, the soldiers of Company M, located in Aurora, Missouri, prior to the war, were spread among the three companies of the newly formed 130th Machine Gun Battalion.

Prior to World War I, Company B, 3rd Missouri Infantry Regiment was located in Boonville, Missouri, although the regiment's home was considered Kansas City. The regiment served during the Mexican Border Campaign, receiving its release from federal service on September 26, 1916. It was again called to duty in World War I, and on September 29, 1917, the 3rd Missouri Infantry Regiment was consolidated with the 6th Missouri Infantry Regiment to form the 140th Infantry Regiment under the 35th Division. Prior to the regiment's deployment overseas, it received intensive training at Camp Doniphan in Fort Sill, Oklahoma.

Louis Eoff Dettwiler was born in Jefferson County, Missouri, on December 20, 1889. He began his military career after enlisting in Company A, 2nd Missouri Infantry in Carthage, Missouri, in 1908. He rose to the rank of first lieutenant in 1913 and went on to serve as first lieutenant with the company during the Mexican Border Campaign. During World War I, he was transferred to Company A, 128th Machine Gun Battalion in October 1917, which prior to the war was known as Company A, 2nd Missouri Infantry Regiment.

Lt. Louis Dettwiler of Carthage was discharged from Company A, 128th Machine Gun Battalion for reasons of disability in April 1918, shortly before the regiment departed Camp Doniphan, Oklahoma, bound for overseas service in World War I. Dettwiler passed away from influenza/pneumonia on December 16, 1918, and was laid to rest in Park Cemetery in Carthage. Prior to his death, he was employed as a druggist with the Wells Drug Company in Carthage. When he registered for the Selective Service Act on September 12, 1918, he was listed as "nervous" under disqualifying disabilities.

A 22-year-old Harry S. Truman is pictured in 1906 while dressed in the uniform of the Missouri National Guard. On June 14, 1905, Truman enlisted as a private in the newly formed Battery B, 2nd Missouri Field Artillery in Kansas City, with whom he served until 1911. The future president would go on to serve in World War I and retire at the rank of colonel from the Officers' Reserve Corps in January 1953.

During World War I, Truman reenlisted in the Missouri National Guard and was federalized as a member of Battery D, 129th Field Artillery of the 35th Division. Promoted to the rank of captain and assuming command of the battery, accounts indicate Truman maintained a strict adherence to discipline and high military standards but was fair to his subordinates and earned their respect as a fair and competent leader. Although his battery of 200 men experienced fierce combat during the war, they suffered no casualties.

Following his service in World War I, Col. Paul Hunt helped establish American Legion Post 5 and served as mayor of Jefferson City. In the late 1920s, he resigned his position as assistant adjutant general of the Missouri National Guard to serve as chief of hatcheries for the state's Game and Fish Department. The 66-year-old veteran succumbed to heart disease on February 14, 1944, and was laid to rest three days later in the Jefferson Barracks National Cemetery.

Maj. Gen. Peter E. Traub, who commanded the 35th Division during the Meuse-Argonne Offensive, is pictured reviewing soldiers of the 140th Infantry Regiment at Rupt-en-Woëvre in northeastern France on November 18, 1918. According to *History of the Missouri National Guard*, published in 1934, the regiment had 9 officers and 239 enlisted soldiers who were killed or died of wounds during World War I.

Capt. James Claude Kenady was serving as commander of Company K, 140th Infantry Regiment of the 35th Division when, just three weeks shy of his 41st birthday, he died in a military hospital in France on October 17, 1918, two weeks after having been shot through the lung. The remains of the married veteran were initially interred in Nevers, France, but were later returned to Missouri and reinterred in a cemetery in his hometown of Dexter.

A native of Indiana, Claude N. Skelton was employed as a teacher in Dexter when he was drafted to serve in Company H, 6th Missouri Infantry Regiment. The Missouri National Guard unit was federalized in World War I, and Skelton became a lieutenant in Company K, 140th Infantry Regiment. During World War I, Skelton was promoted to captain after his commander, Capt. James Kenady, died from wounds received in the Meuse-Argonne Offensive. Skelton later retired to the St. Louis area after a 40-year career as an educator.

Clarence Gillette Smith of Dexter is pictured in 1917 as a young second lieutenant at Camp Clark while his federalized Missouri National Guard company prepared to depart for training at Camp Doniphan, Oklahoma. He served overseas during World War I with Company K, 140th Infantry Regiment. The married veteran passed away at the VA hospital in Indianapolis in 1954. He was only 61 years old and was laid to rest in his native state of Indiana.

Capt. Rolla B. Holt of Kansas City was serving as commanding officer of Company I, 140th Infantry Regiment when he died during the Meuse-Argonne Offensive on September 28, 1918. The veteran's remains were returned to Missouri and interred in Mount Washington Cemetery in Independence in 1921. At the time of his death, Holt was married and the father of several children.

Carl E. Phenix was born in 1897 and living in Poplar Bluff when he enlisted in Company M, 6th Missouri Infantry Regiment of the Missouri National Guard on June 16, 1917. The regiment consolidated with the 3rd Missouri Infantry Regiment during World War I to form the 140th Infantry Regiment of the 35th Division. During the war, the 140th participated in several major engagements, including the deadly Meuse-Argonne Offensive. Following his discharge in 1919, Phenix returned to Missouri and married in 1922. He died on April 22, 1972, and was laid to rest in Jefferson Barracks National Cemetery; his wife, Sylvia, joined him in rest the following year.

Chaplain Evan Alexander Edwards served as the regimental chaplain and official historian for the 140th Infantry Regiment—a federalized National Guard regiment—during World War I. He compiled a detailed chronicle of the regiment's activities during the war in his book *From Doniphan to Verdun*, which was published in 1920.

Clifford Porth had already spent several years in the Missouri National Guard when he was mobilized for service during World War I. He later served with the 815th Pioneer Infantry. After the war, he returned to Jefferson City and became co-owner of the jewelry store opened by his father. In 1919, Porth was present for the dedication of the Meuse-Argonne American Cemetery near Romagne, France, which was attended by Gen. John J. Pershing. In May 1920, Porth displayed in the window of his jewelry business photographs taken during the cemetery's dedication.

Jay Golden Hollingsworth was born in Lexington, Missouri, in 1890. The 26-year-old was inducted into Company A, 6th Missouri Infantry Regiment of the Missouri National Guard on June 4, 1917. The 6th Missouri was combined with the 3rd Missouri and became the 140th Infantry Regiment during World War I. Private Hollingsworth was assigned to Company A, 140th Infantry and served overseas from April 25, 1918, to April 28, 1919. He was slightly wounded on September 27, 1918, during the Meuse-Argonne Offensive. The veteran passed away in 1931 at only 40 years old and is interred at Mount Muncie Cemetery in Lansing, Kansas.

Vincent Kulage joined the Missouri National Guard's Company C, 1st Infantry Regiment in St. Louis on June 21, 1916. The following year, on August 5, 1917, the entire National Guard was drafted into federal service for World War I. The 1st Infantry trained for several weeks at Camp Clark before further combat training at Camp Doniphan, Oklahoma. While in Oklahoma, the 1st Regiment merged with the 5th Missouri Infantry Regiment to form the 138th Infantry. Kulage served overseas with the regiment from May 3, 1918, to April 27, 1919, and was wounded on November 3, 1918, when he was shot through his left calf during a drive against German positions.

Soldiers from 1st Battalion, 139th Infantry Regiment are unrolling their packs in preparation for an inspection while in training at Camp Doniphan on the Fort Sill Reservation near Lawton, Oklahoma, in late 1917. While at Camp Doniphan, the 4th Missouri Infantry Regiment was consolidated with the 2nd Missouri Infantry Regiment to form the 139th Infantry Regiment. The regiment deployed to Europe in support of World War I in the spring of 1918. The combat-hardened regiment returned home and was discharged at Fort Riley, Kansas, in May 1919, with 323 soldiers killed and 1,166 wounded.

The regimental colors of the 140th Infantry Regiment are pictured in this photograph taken shortly after World War I. The 140th Infantry was formed through the consolidation of the 3rd Missouri Infantry Regiment and the 6th Missouri Infantry Regiment and fought under the 35th Division in France during the war. One of these regimental flags is kept at the Museum of Missouri Military History in Jefferson City.

Maj. William B. Robertson of St. Louis became a member of the US Army Air Service—the forerunner to the Air Force—and spent his entire World War I service in stateside training. After the war, he was an aviation pioneer in the St. Louis area and one of two St. Louis residents who selected the site for Lambert Field, in addition to being the first to land a plane there. Robertson served as the first commander of the Missouri National Guard's 110th Observation Squadron and was a financial backer of the 1927 transatlantic flight of Charles Lindbergh. (Museum of Missouri Military History.)

During World War I, the JN-4 Curtiss "Jenny" served the US Army Air Service as a reliable trainer. Many young men who had flown and worked around the plane during the war, including Maj. William B. Robertson of St. Louis, were impressed by its ease of use and capabilities. After the war, surplus Jennys were readily available and affordable, which is why Robertson and the officers of the 110th Observation Squadron of the 35th Division (Missouri National Guard) purchased one for training when the squadron was established in the early 1920s. (Museum of Missouri Military History.)

Three

Training the Military

Missouri National Guard troops are pictured during training at Camp Clark in the years prior to World War I. Established in 1908 as the State Rifle Range, it was officially named Camp Clark following the death of former Adj. Gen. Harvey C. Clark in 1921. During World War I, Camp Clark was used as a mobilization point for many troops from the state; however, the federal government was offered use of the camp as an alternative to the overcrowded Camp Doniphan, Oklahoma, and Camp Funston, Kansas. Representatives from Missouri stressed that Camp Clark had excellent sanitation, an abundance of water, and accommodated 10,000 state troops without crowding.

A color guard is featured on the parade grounds at Jefferson Barracks in this real-photo postcard from World War I. Jefferson Barracks was the first permanent military installation west of the Mississippi River. During World War I, it gained the reputation as one of the toughest infantry camps in the United States. Despite the intense training regimen, many of the soldiers who served at the St. Louis–area post boasted of the kind treatment they received from organizations such as the YMCA and Knights of Columbus.

For soldiers traveling to the bustling Jefferson Barracks and those departing for overseas assignments following completion of their training, one mode of transportation used was trains operated by the St. Louis & Iron Mountain Railroad. The company's railroad depot was built on the Jefferson Barracks along the Mississippi River in 1902 and stood until it was demolished in the 1980s. On May 15, 1917, soldiers preparing to depart the post witnessed the death of James T. Parker, a railroad agent who became pinned between two troop cars while supervising the loading of troop trains.

Deploying troops are pictured in 1917 preparing to board trains for service overseas after completing their training at Jefferson Barracks. During World War I, newspapers reported alleged "immoral conditions" around the post, including saloonkeepers selling alcohol to soldiers who were in uniform despite a War Department edict prohibiting such sales. Some sneaky saloonkeepers, in an effort to thwart the legal liquor sales requirement, reportedly placed civilian clothing in convenient locations near their establishments so that soldiers could pull it over their uniforms before purchasing alcohol.

Jefferson Barracks, located in South County, St. Louis, became the largest induction site in the United States following the formal declaration of war on April 6, 1917. This postcard printed by Curt Teich & Company during World War I captures a large group of recently trained soldiers waiting to board trains to make the trip to the East Coast, where troop ships would be waiting to transport them across the Atlantic to the war raging overseas.

Members of Company B, 314th Engineer Regiment are featured in this photograph taken in 1918. The regiment was under the command and control of the 89th Division and was principally comprised of men drawn from locations throughout Missouri. After receiving training at Camp Funston, Kansas, the regiment deployed to France in the spring of 1918. Company B participated in a number of major engagements of the war, with 7 soldiers killed and 24 wounded or gassed.

Cadets attending the former Kemper Military School in Boonville participated in an intense regimen of academic, athletic, leadership, and military-oriented training and activities. Those in the school's Reserve Officer Training Corps program were required to procure uniforms from the school's quartermaster that were nearly identical to those used by the American Expeditionary Forces in Europe during World War I, including trench caps and wrapped leggings.

The former Kemper Military School in Boonville helped prepare many young men who went on to serve in leadership capacities during World War I. In the years following the war, the school not only continued to provide boys and young men with an academic education, but offered training on various weapons that had been used during World War I, such as the Stokes mortar, M1916 37mm, and M1917 Browning machine guns.

Since its founding in 1890, the Missouri Military Academy in Mexico, Missouri, has provided academic and leadership training that prepared cadets for service in the military. During the summer of 1918, eight cadets and an instructor from the academy attended Reserve Officers' Training Camp at Fort Sheridan, Illinois, receiving the same instruction as soldiers preparing to deploy overseas. The intent of the training was to provide the group with the knowledge to return to Mexico and increase the military efficiency of the academy.

Sandford Sellers Sr. was solicited in 1880 to serve as coprincipal of the institution that became Wentworth Military Academy in Lexington. During his 58 years with the academy, he served in several capacities, eventually becoming president. He ushered in many important changes such as having the academy recognized as a Missouri National Guard post in 1898. He trained scores of cadets who went on to serve in World War I; all three of his sons served.

Ovid Sellers was the oldest son of Col. Sandford Sellers and was raised on the campus of Wentworth Military Academy. During World War I, he served overseas as a chaplain with the US Army. Following his military service, he continued to pursue his education by earning a PhD from Johns Hopkins University. He later became a renowned Biblical scholar, participating in several archaeological expeditions, and was the first person to photograph the cave where the famed Dead Sea Scrolls were discovered. (Wentworth Military Museum.)

Sandford Sellers Jr. was the second oldest of the three sons of Sandford Sellers Sr. During World War I, he was commissioned a captain in the infantry. Following training at Fort Sill, Oklahoma, he was assigned to a machine-gun battalion with the 89th Division, with whom he deployed overseas in late May 1918. After the war, he reunited with his family, spent several years as superintendent at Wentworth Military Academy, earned his master's degree, and later became superintendent of Morgan Park Military Academy in Chicago.

James M. Sellers was a former cadet at Wentworth Military Academy, an institution his father helped establish. The youngest of the three Sellers sons, he was wounded while serving as an officer in the Marine Corps during World War I, earning a Distinguished Service Cross and two Silver Star Medals. After the war, he went on to serve Wentworth Military Academy in the positions of commandant, superintendent, and president.

Mechanical Instruction Building, Military Section of the Rahe Auto & Tractor School, North Kansas City, Mo. Main Civilian Section is Located at Twenty-second and Oak Streets, Kansas City, Mo.

The period of World War I demonstrated that Kansas City was at the forefront of automotive education, primarily because of the existence of Sweeney Automotive and Tractor School in addition to Rahe's Auto and Tractor School. Founded in 1917 by Henry J. Rahe, who had at one time been in partnership with Emory Sweeney, Rahe's Auto and Tractor School was located in north Kansas City and helped train mechanics for the growing automotive industry.

VIEW OF PART OF THE MACHINE SHOP IN THE RAHE AUTO & TRACTOR SCHOOL, KANSAS CITY, MO. THOUSANDS OF DOLLARS' WORTH OF UP-TO-DATE MACHINERY FOR STUDENTS TO PRACTICE ON.

Rahe's Auto and Tractor School established an Army Division to train mechanics for World War I. The school closed within a few years, following the end of the war, and the building was later used for other purposes. It was demolished in the mid-1960s so that the Crown Center could be constructed. The 80-year-old Henry Rahe, the school's founder, died in Kansas City in 1958.

The Sweeney Automotive and Tractor School in Kansas City was established in 1908 by Emory Sweeney in a rented building and had only five students. Enrollment quickly grew, though, to more than 7,100 in 1919. Sweeney later constructed this 10-story building that boasted 12 acres of floor space. During World War I, he secured a government contract to teach mechanical skills to enlisted men; however, the school's demise came with the stock market crash of 1929. The building that formerly housed the school still stands south of Union Station.

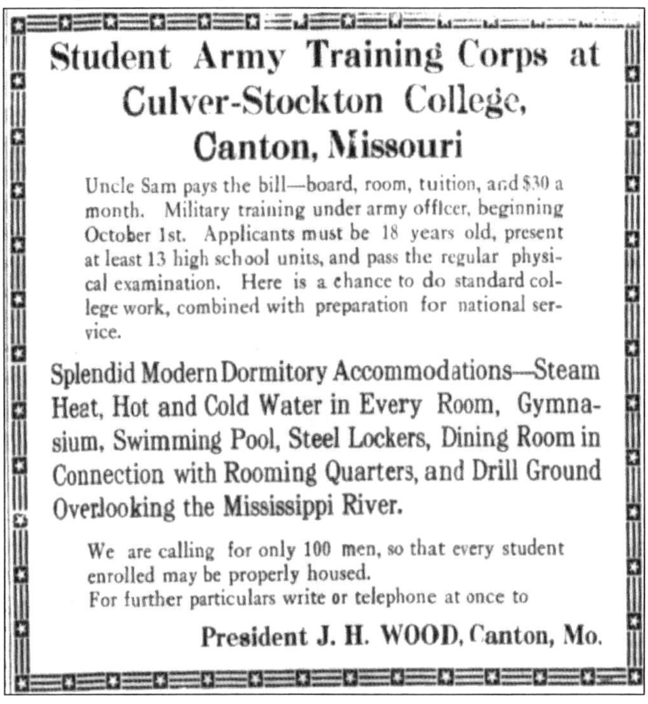

The Student Army Training Corps (SATC) was established during World War I to extend to colleges and universities throughout the United States an opportunity to contribute to the war effort. Jointly administered by the military and each participating university, the program was a combination of a learning atmosphere and military training that prepared trainees and draftees for the various trades needed in the war. Culver-Stockton College in Canton promoted its participation in the SATC in this advertisement from the September 25, 1918, *Clarence Courier* of Clarence, Missouri.

Authorized under the Selective Service Act of 1917, the Student Army Training Corps was able to use the faculty and facilities of higher education institutions throughout the United States to prepare men for service in World War I in such technical and vocational specialties as radio operators, machinists, and mechanics. The program was dissolved following the signing of the armistice on November 11, 1918. Participating in the program were a number of colleges and universities in Missouri, including Washington University, which ran this advertisement in the August 13, 1918, *St. Louis Star and Times.*

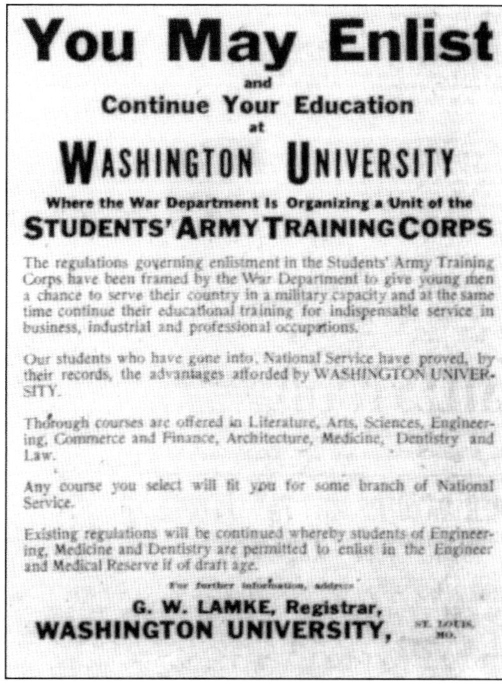

The property for Swope Park, which is Kansas City's largest park at 1,805 acres, was donated by the late Thomas H. Swope. In the years prior to and during World War I, the park was utilized by the Missouri National Guard to conduct training exercises and hold rifle tournaments. Additionally, on August 29, 1918, a "Flying Circus" comprised of nine airplanes from a British-American squadron provided a demonstration of aerial maneuvers and stunts in the park, showing a crowd of more than 100,000 the types of aircraft being used by American, British, French, and Italian aviators in World War I.

Organized at Camp Funston, Kansas, in September 1917, the 89th Division became a national Army division in World War I with Maj. Gen. Leonard Wood as its initial commander. The soldiers of the division came from Kansas, Missouri, Arizona, Colorado, Nebraska, New Mexico, and South Dakota—thus inspiring the name Middle West Division. When flipped, the black "W" on the insignia of the 89th Division becomes an "M," and together, "MW" represents "Midwest."

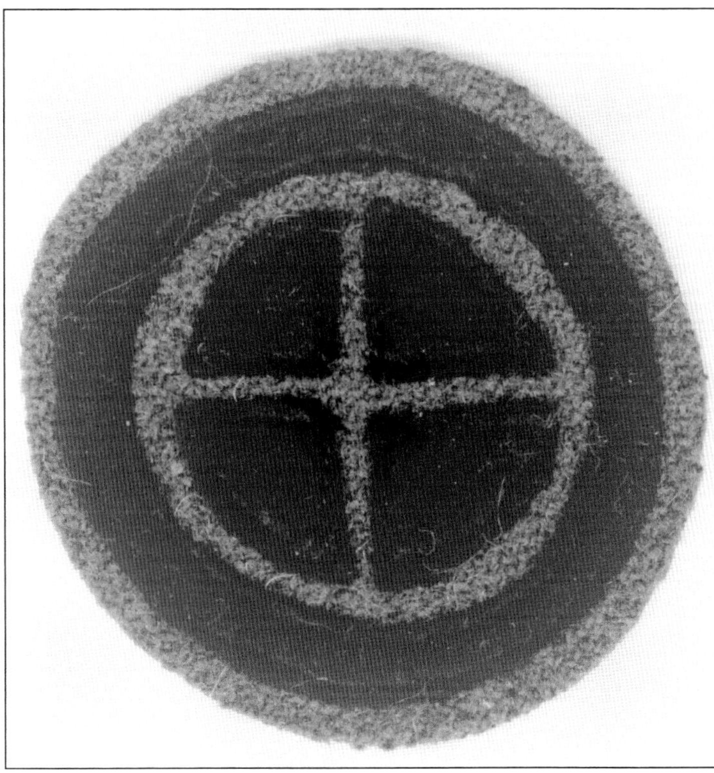

This shoulder patch was worn by a soldier who served in the 35th Infantry Division in World War I. The symbol of the division is a Santa Fe cross set within a wagon wheel. During World War I, the division was initially formed from National Guard units in Nebraska, Kansas, and Missouri. These states were in the vicinity of the historic Santa Fe Trail, which became the primary inspiration for the design of the division's patch.

Four

CALL TO THE COLORS

A 22-year-old Shannon Thompson was living in McBaine, Missouri, and employed as a laborer with Boone County when he registered for the military draft for World War I on June 5, 1917. Inducted into the US Army on September 1, 1918, Thompson trained with the 163rd Depot Brigade at Camp Dodge, Iowa; however, the war ended while he was in training and he remained stateside. The widower died in St. Louis on December 29, 1960, and is interred in the city's Greenwood Cemetery—St. Louis's first commercial, nonsectarian cemetery for African Americans.

John E. Schroeder was born in Troy in 1891 and was self-employed as a farmer when he was inducted into the US Army on September 18, 1917. He was assigned to Headquarters Company 354th Infantry of the 89th Division and served overseas from June 4, 1918, to May 22, 1919, as a trumpet player in the regimental band. Following his discharge, he married, and in 1923 began his career as a chiropractor after finishing a course of study in Iowa. Dr. Shroeder passed away on July 12, 1977.

Possessing only an eighth grade education, Eugene Earle Amick Sr. of Bunceton was at one time the youngest bank president in Missouri. During World War I, he was inducted into the US Navy and received his initial training at Great Lakes Naval Training Station in Illinois; however, he spent the largest part of his naval service in the hospital recovering from the Spanish influenza. (Joanne Comer.)

Sixty-two members of the French Foreign Legion visited St. Louis on September 26, 1918. Comprised of 17 nationalities, including Greeks, Swiss, Peruvians, Spanish, and Armenians, the Legionnaires fought alongside Allied forces in Europe during World War I. The legion was visiting St. Louis as part of the Fourth Liberty Loan campaign, encouraging the purchase of war bonds to help fund the war effort.

Barney J. Bradford was one of nearly 370,000 African Americans inducted into the US Army during World War I. The 29-year-old was married and employed as a plasterer in Mexico, Missouri, when he registered for the draft on June 5, 1917. He served overseas as a mechanic in the all-black Headquarters Company, 809th Pioneer Infantry Regiment. The veteran later moved to Jefferson City and was employed by the state Department of Agriculture and the library at Lincoln University. Following his death in 1950, he was laid to rest in Jefferson City National Cemetery. (Pete Oetting.)

In January 1916, Buhal H. Jones, a 22-year-old paper hanger and painter, became an accomplice to the robbery of the money drawer from the Burlington Railroad station in St. Joseph. He was one of three defendants who plead guilty to the crime in April 1916 and was sentenced to two years in the penitentiary; however, Jones received a pardon on March 13, 1917, for good behavior, since he made the decision to enlist in the US Navy on April 10.

Marie Sophia Kammeyer of Concordia, Missouri, received her nursing training at the Lutheran Hospital School of Nursing in St. Louis. On May 5, 1917, she enlisted in the Army Nurse Corps and spent nearly two years overseas assisting the British armed forces at a hospital in Rouem, France, until her discharge on June 17, 1919. Several months later, on November 17, 1919, she married Alvin Stockhaus and later gave birth to two children. The 91-year-old World War I nurse passed away in 1982 and is buried in Cleveland, Ohio. (Museum of Missouri Military History.)

Paul A. Hamilton of Harrisonville is pictured in 1917 while captain of the University of Missouri–Columbia football team. The 21-year-old entered military service at Camp Pike, Arkansas, on January 5, 1918, and attended officers' training school with the 87th Division. He earned his commission as a second lieutenant in the infantry and remained stateside during the remainder of his enlistment, receiving his discharge from the Army in the fall of 1919.

Frank Watts of Enon, Missouri, traveled overseas in World War I aboard the USS *Siboney*. Acquired by the US Navy and commissioned in 1918, the *Siboney*—an 11,298-ton transport—set sail with Watts's regiment on September 30, 1918, and arrived in France on October 14, 1918. The *Siboney* made six round-trip voyages during the First World War for the purpose of delivering troops to the war zone in Europe. The people onboard were struck hard by the Spanish influenza during her sixth trip, killing 38 men in early October 1918, the same time that Watts was onboard.

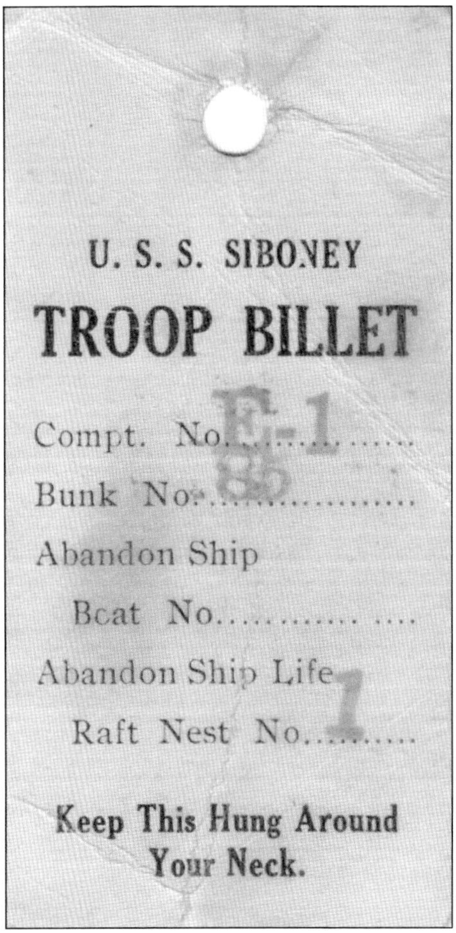

Pvt. Frank Watts sent this photograph to his wife during World War I, which shows the often dark and cramped conditions the doughboys experienced in their wartime travels. One soldier's recounting of his personal experience aboard such a vessel noted that the troops making the transatlantic voyage were required to wear life vests while eating meals and also while sleeping. Additionally, they were awakened any time they were traveling in waters frequented by submarines in case the ship was attacked and the abandon ship order was given.

Soldiers traveling overseas via a troop transport were issued billet tags such as the one pictured here that belonged to Frank Watts. This tag denoted the bunk in which Private Watts, a soldier of Company M, 130th Infantry Regiment, was assigned during his voyage in addition to the location of the life raft he would use in the event that an abandon ship order was given. These tags, generally discarded after the completion of the soldier's voyage, are now a relatively rare artifact from the war.

William Borgmeyer is pictured with his wife, Elizabeth, shortly after receiving his discharge at Camp Funston, Kansas, in 1919. Borgmeyer enlisted in the US Army in 1915 and went on to serve with Battery F, 6th Field Artillery Regiment in the Mexican Border Campaign. During World War I, he became a member of the 1st Division and was gassed in the Meuse-Argonne Offensive. (Roman Borgmeyer.)

The World War I Victory Medal was awarded for qualifying service in the armed forces between April 6, 1917, and April 1, 1920. For those serving with the US Army, there were five Army Battle Clasps authorized with the medal. This particular medal once belonged to Osage County veteran William Borgmeyer, who, as denoted by the battle clasps, participated in all five campaigns of the war.

WAR DEPARTMENT

LOCAL BOARD FOR

Local Board for the County of Miller State of Mo.

Tuscumbia, Mo.

OFFICIAL BUSINESS

PENALTY FOR PRIVATE USE, $300

TUSCUMBIA FEB 5 PM 1918 MO.

Robert J. Edgmond

Henley

Mo.

c3—5130

A 21-year-old Robert Jack Edgmond was required to register for the draft on June 5, 1917, claiming exemption from service since he provided support for his father, mother, and sister while working on the family farm near Henley, Missouri. Under the Selective Service Act of 1917, Edgmond's local board in Miller County had the responsibility for determining the eligibility of draftees and examining exemptions. The outcome of this process was shared on registration classification postcards, the front of which is pictured.

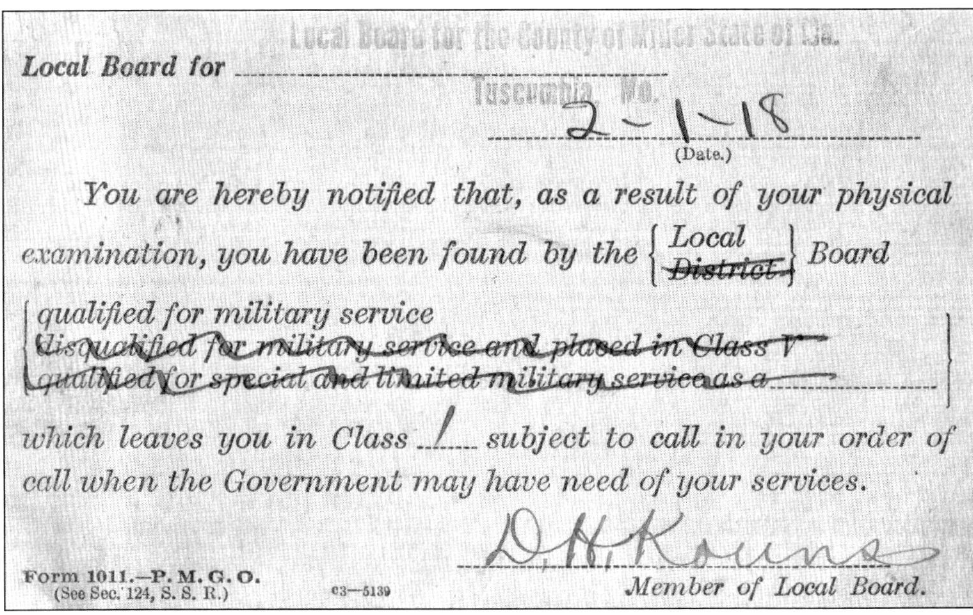

Local Board for the County of Miller State of Mo.

Local Board for Tuscumbia, Mo.

2-1-18
(Date.)

You are hereby notified that, as a result of your physical examination, you have been found by the {Local ~~District~~} Board

qualified for military service
~~disqualified for military service and placed in Class V~~
~~qualified for special and limited military service as a~~

which leaves you in Class 1 *subject to call in your order of call when the Government may have need of your services.*

D. H. Kouns
Member of Local Board.

Form 1011.—P. M. G. O.
(See Sec. 124, S. S. R.)

c3—5139

Robert Edgmond received from his local draft board a registration classification postcard, the back of which noted that on February 1, 1918, he was considered Class I, meaning both eligible and liable for military service. He was inducted into the US Army on July 21, 1918, and became a mechanic with the Supply Company of the 29th Field Artillery, which was struck hard with Spanish influenza while stationed at Camp Funston. The war ended before it could be sent overseas.

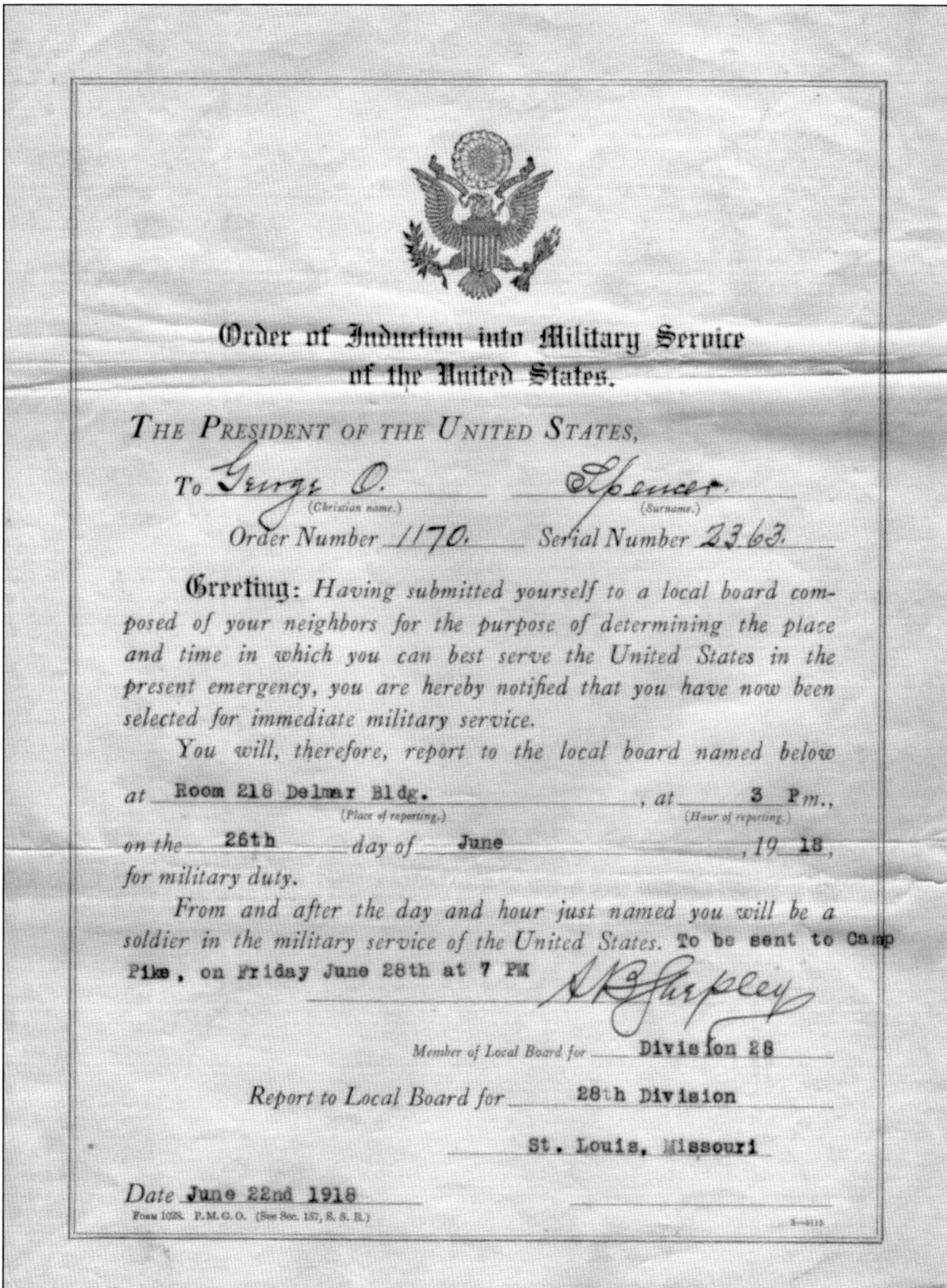

Order of Induction into Military Service of the United States.

The President of the United States,

To George O. Spencer
(Christian name.) (Surname.)

Order Number 1170 Serial Number 2363

Greeting: *Having submitted yourself to a local board composed of your neighbors for the purpose of determining the place and time in which you can best serve the United States in the present emergency, you are hereby notified that you have now been selected for immediate military service.*

You will, therefore, report to the local board named below at Room 218 Delmar Bldg. *, at* 3 Pm.,
(Place of reporting.) (Hour of reporting.)

on the 26th *day of* June *, 19* 18,
for military duty.

From and after the day and hour just named you will be a soldier in the military service of the United States. To be sent to Camp Pike, on Friday June 28th at 7 PM

S K Sharpley

Member of Local Board for Division 28

Report to Local Board for 28th Division

St. Louis, Missouri

Date June 22nd 1918

Form 1028. P.M.G.O. (See Sec. 157, S. S. R.)

George O. Spencer of Stanton, Missouri, received his Order of Induction into Military Service of the United States from his local draft board in St. Louis, ordering him to report on June 25, 1918. Spencer was inducted into the US Army on June 28, 1918, and completed his initial training at Camp Pike, Arkansas. He went on to serve as a private overseas from August 24, 1918, to April 23, 1919, with both the 161st and 137th Infantry Regiments.

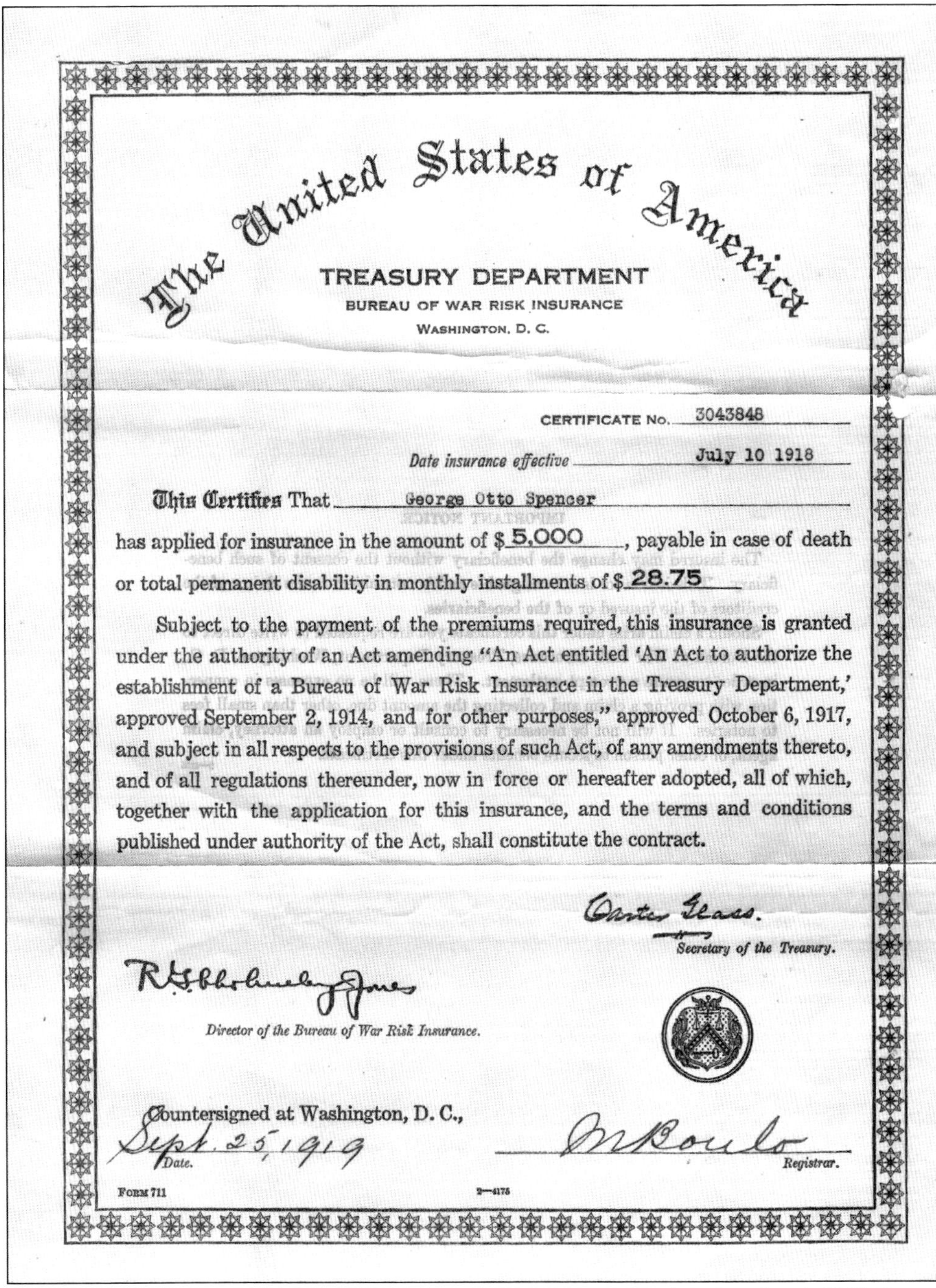

The United States of America

TREASURY DEPARTMENT

BUREAU OF WAR RISK INSURANCE

WASHINGTON, D. C.

CERTIFICATE No. 3043848

Date insurance effective July 10 1918

This Certifies That George Otto Spencer

has applied for insurance in the amount of $5,000, payable in case of death or total permanent disability in monthly installments of $28.75

Subject to the payment of the premiums required, this insurance is granted under the authority of an Act amending "An Act entitled 'An Act to authorize the establishment of a Bureau of War Risk Insurance in the Treasury Department,' approved September 2, 1914, and for other purposes," approved October 6, 1917, and subject in all respects to the provisions of such Act, of any amendments thereto, and of all regulations thereunder, now in force or hereafter adopted, all of which, together with the application for this insurance, and the terms and conditions published under authority of the Act, shall constitute the contract.

Carter Glass.

Secretary of the Treasury.

Director of the Bureau of War Risk Insurance.

Countersigned at Washington, D. C.,

Sept. 25, 1919

Date.

Registrar.

FORM 711 2—4175

As a provision of Article IV of the War Risk Insurance Act approved on October 6, 1917, George Spencer was able to purchase between $1,000 and $10,000 in life insurance payable in the event of his death or permanent disability; the soldier chose $5,000 in coverage, as noted on this form. The insurance was granted and the premium calculated without regard to the level of risk incurred by the service member making the application under the program. There was also a provision made after the war that allowed the service member to convert the insurance to a permanent policy.

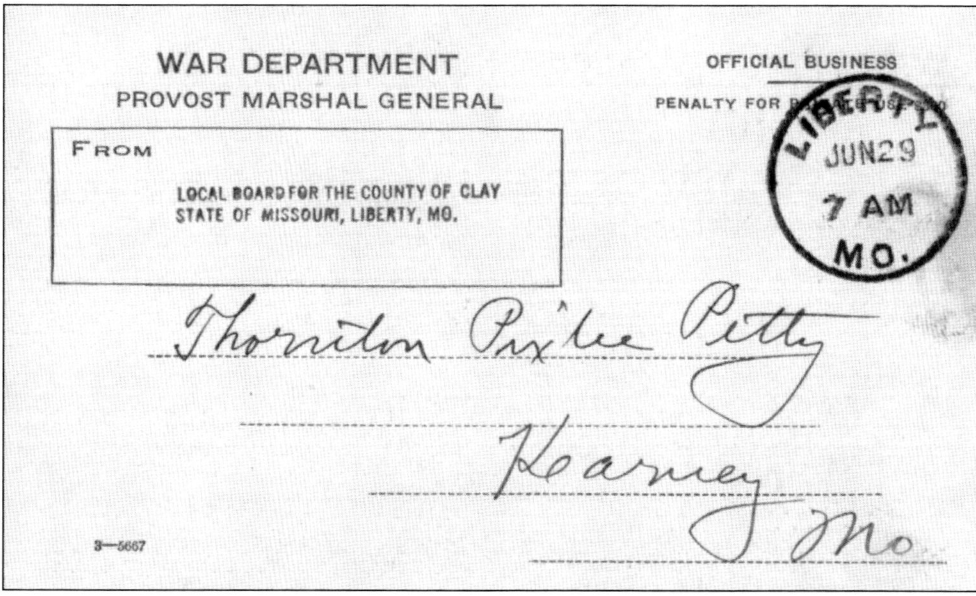
WAR DEPARTMENT
PROVOST MARSHAL GENERAL

OFFICIAL BUSINESS
PENALTY FOR

FROM
LOCAL BOARD FOR THE COUNTY OF CLAY
STATE OF MISSOURI, LIBERTY, MO.

LIBERTY
JUN 29
7 AM
MO.

Thornton Pixlee Petty
Kearney
Mo

3—5667

Thornton P. Petty was living in Kearney, Missouri, when he received a postcard from his local draft board in Clay County, the front of which is pictured here. The postcard was dated June 29, 1918, advising him that he would be called to military service at Jefferson Barracks during the five-day period beginning July 5, 1918.

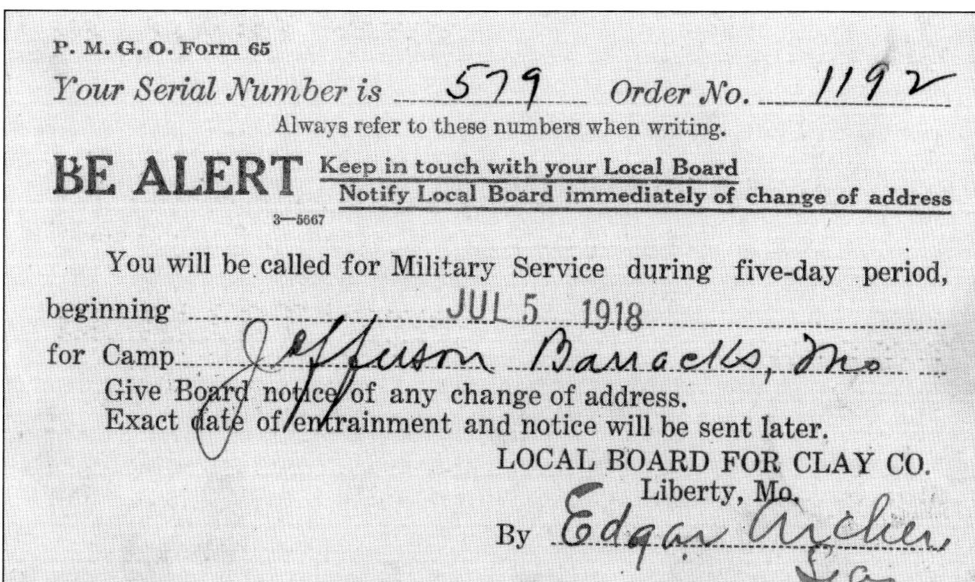
P. M. G. O. Form 65

Your Serial Number is 579 *Order No.* 1192
Always refer to these numbers when writing.

BE ALERT Keep in touch with your Local Board
Notify Local Board immediately of change of address

3—5667

You will be called for Military Service during five-day period, beginning JUL 5 1918
for Camp Jefferson Barracks, Mo
Give Board notice of any change of address.
Exact date of entrainment and notice will be sent later.

LOCAL BOARD FOR CLAY CO.
Liberty, Mo.
By Edgar Archer
Secy

As indicated on the back of this postcard received by Thornton Petty, he was called to service and inducted into the US Army on July 6, 1918. Following his initial training at Camp MacArthur, Texas, he served overseas with Company B, 163rd Infantry from August 23, 1918, to June 14, 1919. He received his discharge more than a year later, on July 25, 1919.

William Thomas Burns was born in Springfield, Missouri, and first entered the US Army in 1913. During World War I, Lieutenant Burns was assigned to the 366th Infantry Regiment of the 92nd Division—known as Buffalo Soldiers—and served overseas from August 15, 1918, to February 28, 1919. He was twice wounded in action. The combat veteran died January 27, 1965, and was laid to rest in Glendale Cemetery in Des Moines, Iowa. (Museum of Missouri Military History.)

Born in St. Louis in 1897, Leslie Brauks was inducted into the US Army on March 9, 1897. He went on to spend his entire period of service with an air squadron at Scott Field, Illinois (now Scott Air Force Base), and later at Wilbur Wright Field, Ohio (now Wright-Patterson AFB), supporting planes such as the Curtiss JN-3D "Jenny" used to train pilots. After the war, he was employed as a tool maker for an automotive manufacturing company in the St. Louis area.

A 1915 graduate of Carthage High School, Wilbur Fisk Maring was attending the University of Missouri in Columbia when he was inducted into Company F, 4th Regiment of the Missouri National Guard. The unit was later federalized under the 35th Division, and Fisk went on to serve as a machine-gun officer overseas with the 137th Infantry during the war. He was recalled to active duty in World War II and later served in the Korean War, retiring at the rank of colonel in 1957. He is pictured here as one of the commanding officers of the University of Missouri's ROTC program after World War I.

Elmer Seals was born in Kansas City in 1895 and was inducted into the US Army in Detroit, Michigan, on September 11, 1918. At the time of his induction, he worked as a laborer at Buick Motor Company in Flint, Michigan. He initially trained with the 160th Depot Brigade at Camp Custer, Michigan, but was transferred to Company C, 448th Reserve Labor Battalion on November 21, 1918, also at Camp Custer. Since World War I was a period of segregation for the military, most African American soldiers were limited in the roles they could fill, typically assigned to menial positions in labor battalions. The 92-year-old veteran died in Kansas City in 1987 and is buried in Leavenworth National Cemetery. (Museum of Missouri Military History.)

A number of Missouri soldiers served with the 89th Division as members of the 314th Engineer Regiment, some of whom are pictured constructing barbed wire entanglements near Bouillonville, France, on September 30, 1918. The 314th had recently taken part in the St. Mihiel Offensive and was busy constructing the barriers in front of new trenches. The 49 officers and 1,005 soldiers of the 314th returned to the United States aboard the USS *Montana* in May 1919. (Museum of Missouri Military History.)

Pictured is an entrance to one of the dugouts in Bouillonville, France, similar to those encountered by a number of Missouri soldiers during World War I. This dugout is where Sgt. Harry J. Adams, a Kansas soldier in Company K, 353rd Infantry Regiment of the 89th Division, single-handedly captured 375 German prisoners during the St. Mihiel Offensive in September 1918, armed only with a revolver. For his actions, Adams was awarded the Distinguished Service Cross. (Museum of Missouri Military History.)

Soldiers of the 354th Infantry Regiment crowd the docks at Brest, Germany, awaiting their opportunity to board the *Leviathan* for return home. While serving with the Army of Occupation following the armistice, many soldiers of the regiment availed themselves of the educational offerings to obtain a basic grammar school education. Others were involved in athletic events, participating in inter-regimental baseball, basketball, soccer, and football games.

Many of the Missouri soldiers serving with the 354th Infantry Regiment found that their occupational duties following the armistice also provided breaks for sightseeing in Europe. Soldiers of the regiment had the opportunity to take a trip along the scenic Rhine River and are pictured here while visiting Koblenz, Germany, on April 18, 1919.

The 354th Infantry Regiment was organized as a component of the 89th Division at Camp Funston during World War I and was comprised of many soldiers from Missouri. The regiment was heavily engaged in trench warfare and went on to receive campaign credit for the St. Mihiel Offensive, Meuse-Argonne Offensive, and the Battle of Lorraine. This photograph, taken by a soldier of the 354th Infantry Regiment, shows a "street" in their camp while stationed at Brest, France, in May 1919 as they prepared to return to the United States.

Combat veterans of the 354th Infantry Regiment, along with 177th Infantry Brigade Headquarters, crowded aboard the deck of the USS *Imperator*, setting sail for the United States on May 15, 1919. The *Imperator* was a German commercial liner built in Hamburg in 1910 that was used by the United States after the armistice to transport troops back to the states.

A soldier of the 354th Infantry Regiment took this photograph of the SS *Leviathan* in the harbor of Brest, France, on May 14, 1919. The *Leviathan* was formerly the German liner *Vaterland*, which was seized by the United States early in the war. The *Leviathan* served as a troop transport during the war; at the time this photograph was taken, she was preparing to transport soldiers of the 355th Infantry, 353rd Infantry, and the 340th and 341st Machine Gun Battalions back to the United States.

The 354th Infantry Regiment became part of the Army of Occupation following the armistice of November 11, 1918, and in February 1919 was detached from the 89th Division and assigned to the 3rd Army Troops in Trier, Germany. During their occupational duties, a soldier of the 354th Infantry took this photograph of a storage facility used by the German military to house a zeppelin—a massive airship used for bombing and scouting.

A 27-year-old George Scheperle was inducted into the US Army on September 20, 1917. He joined many other men from Missouri who formed a company under the 89th Division and received their initial training at Camp Funston, Kansas. After serving overseas during World War I, Scheperle returned to his rural home in central Missouri, married, raised three sons, and worked several decades as a farmer and bricklayer.

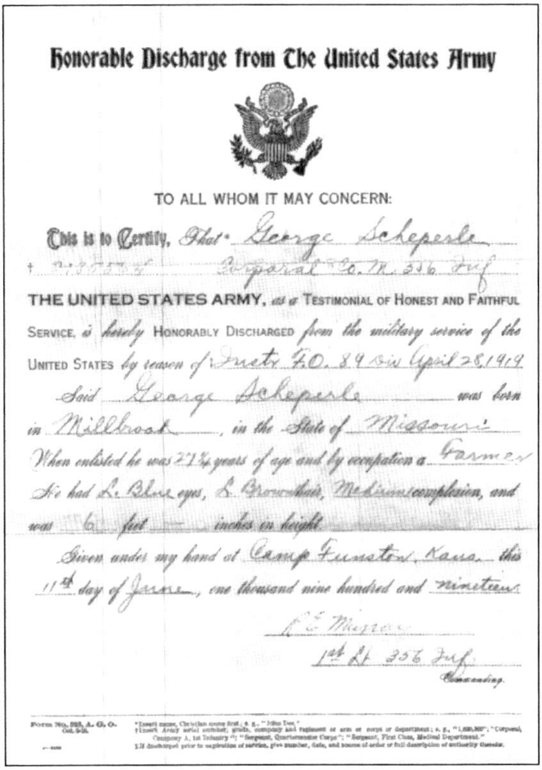

Honorable Discharge from The United States Army

TO ALL WHOM IT MAY CONCERN:

This is to Certify, That George Scheperle

Corporal Co. M. 356 Inf

THE UNITED STATES ARMY, as a TESTIMONIAL OF HONEST AND FAITHFUL SERVICE, is hereby HONORABLY DISCHARGED from the military service of the UNITED STATES by reason of Instr. F.O. 84 Div April 28, 1919

Said George Scheperle was born in Millbrook, in the State of Missouri

When enlisted he was 27 years of age and by occupation a Farmer

He had L. Blue eyes, L. Brown hair, Medium complexion, and was 6 feet — inches in height.

Given under my hand at Camp Funston, Kans. this 11th day of June, one thousand nine hundred and nineteen

R. E. Murray

1st Lt 356 Inf.

Commanding.

World War I discharge papers provide a fount of information on the service of veterans; however, a 1973 fire at the National Personnel Records Center in St. Louis reportedly resulted in the destruction of approximately 80 percent of Army discharge records from 1912 to 1960. Fortunately, many individuals retained copies of their discharges, such as the late George Scheperle of Millbrook (Lohman), who served with Company M, 356th Infantry Regiment during the war.

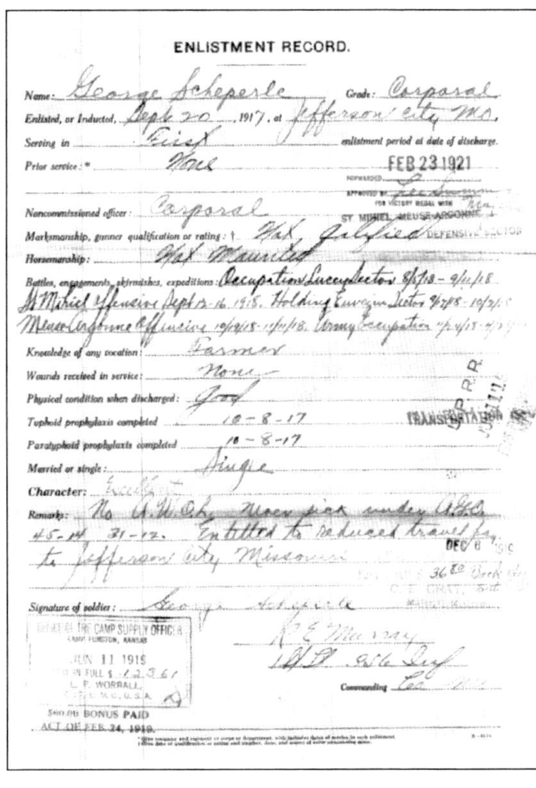

ENLISTMENT RECORD.

Name: George Scheperle Grade: Corporal

Enlisted, or Inducted, Sept 20, 1917, at Jefferson City Mo.

Serving in First enlistment period at date of discharge.

Prior service: None

FEB 23 1921

Noncommissioned officer: Corporal

ST. MIHIEL, MEUSE-ARGONNE

Marksmanship, gunner qualification or rating: Not Qualified

DEFENSIVE SECTOR

Horsemanship: Not Mounted

Battles, engagements, skirmishes, expeditions: Occupation Luceys Sector 8/8/18 – 9/11/18. St Mihiel Offensive Sept 12–16 1918. Holding Euvezin Sector 9/17/18 – 10/2/18. Meuse Argonne Offensive 10/19/18 – 11/11/18. Army Occupation

Knowledge of any vocation: Farmer

Wounds received in service: None

Physical condition when discharged: Good

Typhoid prophylaxis completed 10-8-17

Paratyphoid prophylaxis completed 10-8-17

Married or single: Single

Character: Excellent

Remarks: No A.W.O.L. ... 45-14 31-12. Entitled to reduced travel pay to Jefferson City, Missouri

TRANSPORTATION

Signature of soldier: George Scheperle

CAMP SUPPLY OFFICER CAMP FUNSTON, KANSAS JUN 11 1919 ... L. F. WORRALL

$60.00 BONUS PAID ACT OF FEB. 24, 1919.

R. E. Murray 1st Lt 356 Inf

Commanding

In addition to the retention of records by families, copies of discharge documents for many World War I veterans are available through the Missouri State Archives. Pictured is the reverse side of the discharge document for Cpl. George Scheperle, providing valuable information such as his participation in several campaigns of the war, including the St. Mihiel Offensive and the Meuse-Argonne Offensive.

Five

SUPPORTING AN ARMY

Soldiers pose in St. Louis while preparing to depart for Kansas City on the next step of their military journey aboard the Missouri Pacific Iron Mountain Railroad. In May 1917, the St. Louis, Iron Mountain & Southern Railway merged with the Missouri Pacific. Railroads became greatly stressed during the war, often operating around the clock to move troops and supplies.

The Selective Service Act of 1917 brought thousands of young Missourians into the war effort; however, another group that was drafted into service by the thousands were Missouri mules. During the war, mules were embraced by the Allies since they could carry heavy loads, were surefooted, and could endure harsh conditions. It is estimated that in 1917, there were 90,000 mules serving overseas in support of the war effort. Sadly, many died in combat alongside their handlers.

Mules gained the reputation of being able to drag heavy artillery pieces to forward locations where neither a horse nor vehicle could navigate the mucky conditions. One Missouri firm, Guyton and Harrington of Lathrop, became the largest mule dealership during the war, employing 150 men who cared for 50,000 mules. The company sold 180,000 mules to the British army between 1914 and 1918. During the Boer War in 1901 and 1902, the firm experienced a boom selling horses to the British army.

The Inland Machine Works of St. Louis sought to demonstrate its support of the war effort while at the same time marketing its products by encouraging the purchase of piston rings. According to advertisements appearing in magazines throughout 1918, its patented one-piece piston ring could improve the efficiency of gasoline engines, thus preserving precious fuel that could be used in the war effort. The company closed in 1924.

This capital stock certificate, dated 1897, features the former St. Charles Car Company of St. Charles. Founded in 1873, the company manufactured passenger railcars and streetcars. In 1899, it became one of 13 companies that merged to form the American Car and Foundry Company. During World War I, the American Car and Foundry Company produced a number of items under contract for the government, including artillery shells, caissons, escort wagons, artillery gun mounts, and submarine chasers.

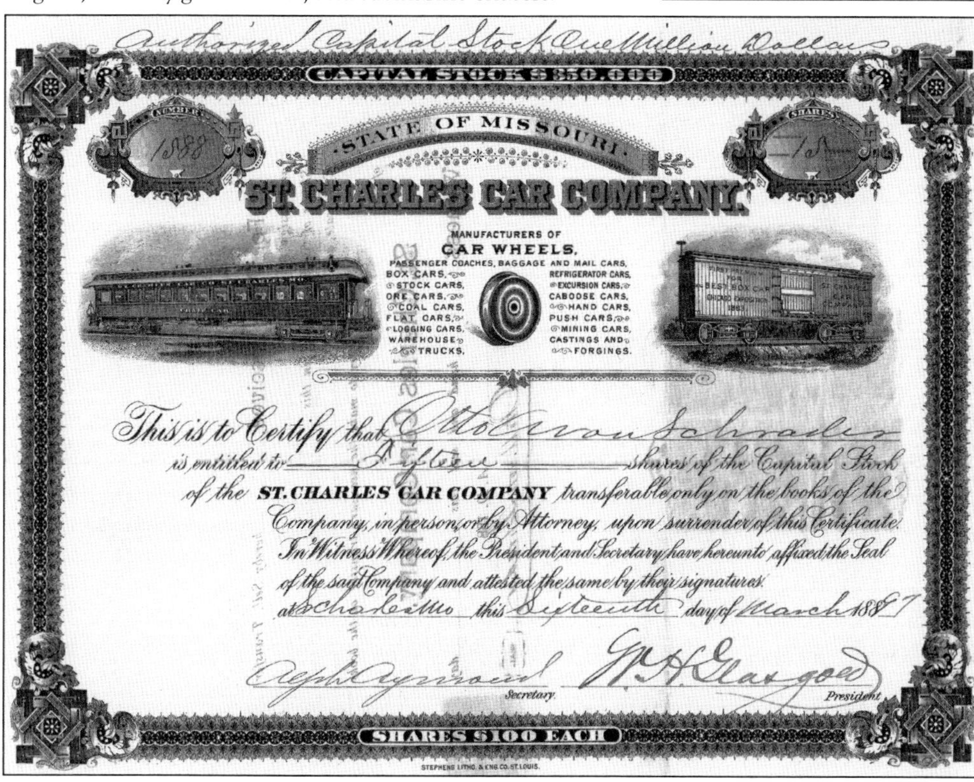

One of the artillery pieces produced by the American Car and Foundry Company during World War I was this 75-mm gun caisson. The employees at the St. Charles Car Company plant not only produced escort wagons, but utilized woodworking equipment to construct chests for the artillery vehicles built in Detroit. Additionally, the foundry at the St. Charles plant produced 2,208 cast-iron stoves used at military bases during the war.

Maj. Gen. Clarence C. Williams, chief of ordnance during World War I, sent a letter in January 1919 to the president of the American Car Company extending his appreciation for "the hearty co-operation and the valuable assistance the Ordnance Department has received from your company in supplying artillery vehicles and artillery ammunition requirements of the Army." This medal was awarded by the company to 7,500 employees who worked diligently to produce munitions and equipment in support of the war effort.

Dr. Max Starkoff, the son of a Civil War surgeon, rose to the occasion in World War I by working to protect the people of St. Louis from the deadly Spanish influenza epidemic of 1918. St. Louis mayor Henry Kiel granted Dr. Starkoff, who was at the time the St. Louis city health commissioner, authority to initiate closures of public spaces in an effort to prevent spread of the flu, which resulted in the closure of schools, playgrounds, theaters, and churches. There were 31,693 cases of influenza reported in St. Louis and 2,883 deaths.

The Spanish influenza pandemic is considered the worst medical crisis in Missouri's history, with the first cases being reported at Jefferson Barracks in 1918. During the pandemic, American Red Cross workers and volunteers, such as those pictured here in St. Louis, provided valuable assistance by producing supplies like surgical dressings and influenza masks in addition to transporting health care personnel and patients.

American Red Cross volunteers, including those in Missouri, wore pins such as these to denote their association with the organization during World War I. Founded in 1881, the Red Cross received its first congressional charter in 1900 and continues in its mission to provide services to members of the US Armed Forces and their families. Despite its small size and funding shortages early in World War I, the Red Cross was able to launch the medical ship SS *Red Cross* to Europe early in the war to provide critical care and treatment to the wounded.

Not only did women from Missouri work in support of the Red Cross Canteen Service, but many went on to serve as nurses with the humanitarian organization. During the war, the Red Cross dispatched doctors and nurses to support wounded Allied troops in addition to setting up 54 hospitals overseas, the majority of which were located in France.

One very active chapter of the American Red Cross during the war was found in St. Charles County. The chapter was officially established on May 24, 1917, and quickly grew in size to an impressive enrollment of 750 members. One of the programs implemented in July 1917 was the creation of a chapter sewing room, where volunteers sewed hospital garments in support of the war effort.

Many women from Missouri became volunteers and were sent overseas with the Red Cross Canteen Service. Throughout the war, the Red Cross operated several canteens near the front lines and served meals and snacks to Allied soldiers from the United States, France, Great Britain, and Italy. The Red Cross notes that during the war, the "canteen service distributed 1.5 million gallons of coffee, 15 million sandwiches, and 11 million cookies, doughnuts, and pies."

Many women from Missouri served on the front lines during World War I through their service in the Salvation Army. One of the most appreciated tasks they performed, in addition to serving coffee, was frying doughnuts. Often, they had to use large shell casings as rolling pins to ensure the doughnuts could be made for the battle-weary troops. National Doughnut Day was started in 1938 in celebration and remembrance of the valuable service provided by these "Doughnut Lassies" during the war.

The Young Men's Christian Association (YMCA) was one of several service organizations that established recreational centers for service members during World War I. Located on military bases and areas where significant numbers of troops were passing through, these buildings were known as "Huts" and provided sites for both recreational activities and religious services. This particular YMCA, one of approximately 4,000 established during World War I, served troops passing through Kansas City.

CANTEEN—SOLDIERS' AND SAILORS' COMMUNITY CLUB

The first Soldiers' and Sailors' Community Club was established at 1305 Walnut Street in downtown Kansas City during World War I. The club was operated as a component of the War Camp Community Service program—a secular social service organization that provided a range of recreational services to service members to boost morale and to keep the troops from getting into any trouble while in training.

NO CHARGE FOR POOL—SOLDIERS' AND SAILORS' COMMUNITY CLUB

The popularity of the Soldiers' and Sailors' Community Club quickly grew, and in late summer 1918, it was visited by 8,000 service members in one week, according to the September 4, 1918, *Leavenworth Times*. The club not only offered accommodations to visiting service members, but also a canteen, games, and music. A club for black troops was later established at Eighteenth and Vine Streets under the authority of the Colored Division of the War Camp Community Service of Kansas City.

As part of the Knights of Columbus War Fund, money was raised to establish buildings on military bases to serve as recreational centers for all military members, regardless of creed. In 1917, this building was erected on Jefferson Barracks in south St. Louis and hosted a number of recreational activities for soldiers stationed at the base or passing through to their next duty assignment. In early 1919, after the end of World War I, the building was purchased by the American Library Association and became an extension for the St. Louis Public Library.

According to the Knights of Columbus Museum, the first and last American military officers to die in World War I were members of the Knights of Columbus (K of C). On the home front, K of C members hosted fundraising drives and provided hospitality at recreational centers under the motto, "Everyone Welcome. Everything Free." Pictured in this real-photo postcard dated May 27, 1919, is the booth operated by the K of C to support troops passing through Union Station in St. Louis.

Many young soldiers utilized the beneficence of the Jewish Welfare Board (JWB). This postcard provided by the JWB was sent by a Missouri soldier returning from his overseas service in World War I informing his family that he was back in camp in the United States. During the war, the JWB not only provided materials such as these postcards, but helped recruit and train rabbis for the military and established Jewish worship facilities.

In addition to the various humanitarian and medical services of the American Red Cross during World War I, it provided postcards such as these for troops to advise their families of their return to the states. This postcard was sent by Thornton Petty, who served overseas with the 163rd Infantry. Petty advised his father in Kearney that he had arrived at Newport News, Virginia, and was heading for demobilization camp.

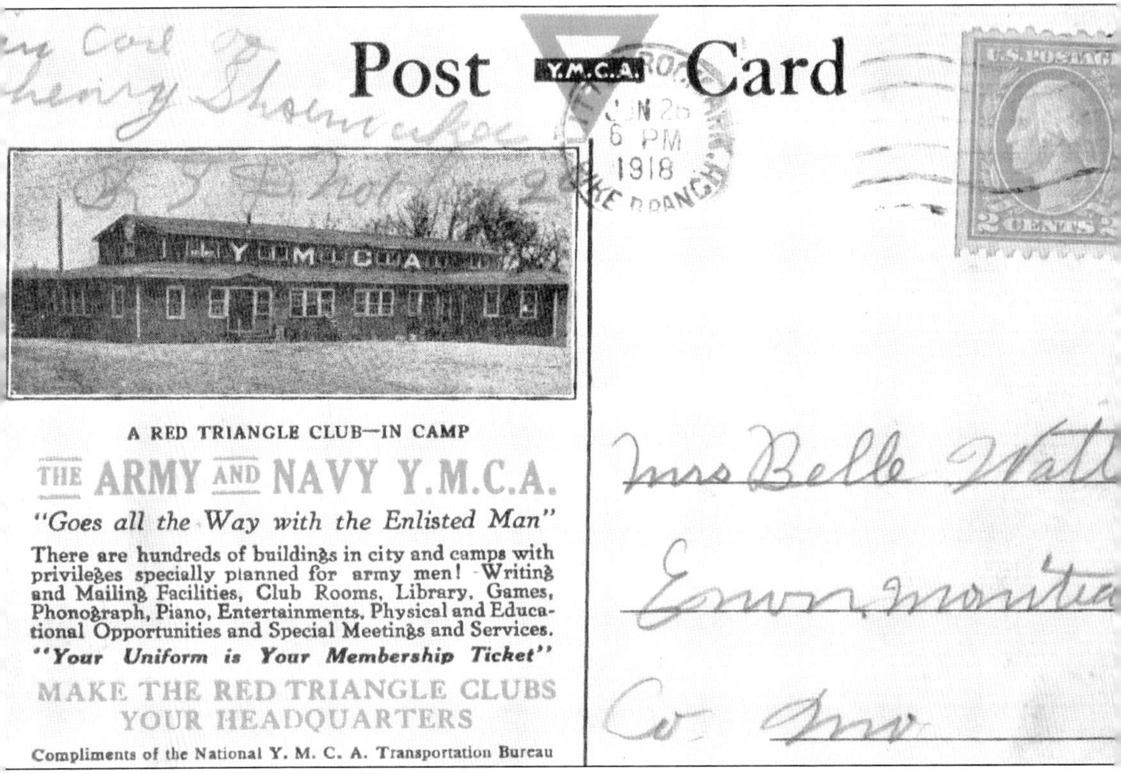

While assigned to the 162nd Depot Brigade at Camp Pike, Arkansas, for his basic training in June 1918, Frank Watts of Enon, Missouri, sent this postcard to his wife, Belle. During World War I, the YMCA established Red Triangle Clubs at a number of military bases as a component of its charitable services, providing writing materials such as this postcard that allowed troops to communicate with their families back home.

Many communities throughout Missouri supported the War Savings Service. As part of the program, citizens pledged to save money wherever possible, purchase war savings stamps, and encourage others in their communities to do the same. Many individuals were issued buttons such as this to denote that they had made the pledge of support.

The likeness of Gen. John J. Pershing, commander of the American Expeditionary Forces, was often used in appeals to the public for their support in the war effort. This poster from the YMCA advertises the United War Work Campaign, which was a joint voluntary effort between several organizations to raise at least $170.5 million in subscriptions and pledges during the week of November 11–18, 1918. The funds raised during the campaign were used to support morale and for recreational activities for US troops. (American Legion Post 5.)

The war resulted in exponential growth for the Red Cross, which grew from 107 local chapters in 1914 to 3,864 in 1918. During the Christmas season of 1918, with the war recently ended, the Red Cross once again called upon the generosity of Americans to assist with relief efforts under a "Roll Call." The poster for this effort was created by designer Ray Greenleaf and features a red cross in the window of a snow-laden cottage, denoting the residents had already responded to the relief effort. (American Legion Post 5.)

Six

THE AMERICAN LEGION

Col. Bennett Champ Clark, left, is pictured with his father, John Beauchamp "Champ" Clark, shortly after returning from his World War I service overseas. While still in France in early 1919, the junior Clark, along with several of his fellow World War I veterans, participated in the Paris Caucus, which became the founding moment for the American Legion. Bennett was the presiding officer at the caucus and was elected the first national commander of the organization. The American Legion was formally established several weeks later, in early May 1919, during meetings held in St. Louis.

The third national convention of the American Legion in Kansas City was advertised as an opportunity for members who had served together in France to reunite with those with whom they had served. The convention featured a number of entertainment activities planned by the community and was also used as the forum to dedicate the site for the new Liberty Memorial.

On July 4, 1919, approximately two months after the constitution of the American Legion was approved at the St. Louis Caucus, the first issue of *The American Legion Weekly* was published. Gen. John J. Pershing noted the magazine would be "the medium of communication throughout the country [that] will more closely unite the already strong bonds of comradeship among the members." Pictured is the September 23, 1921, issue advertising the upcoming third national convention held in Kansas City from October 31 through November 2, 1921. (American Legion Post 5.)

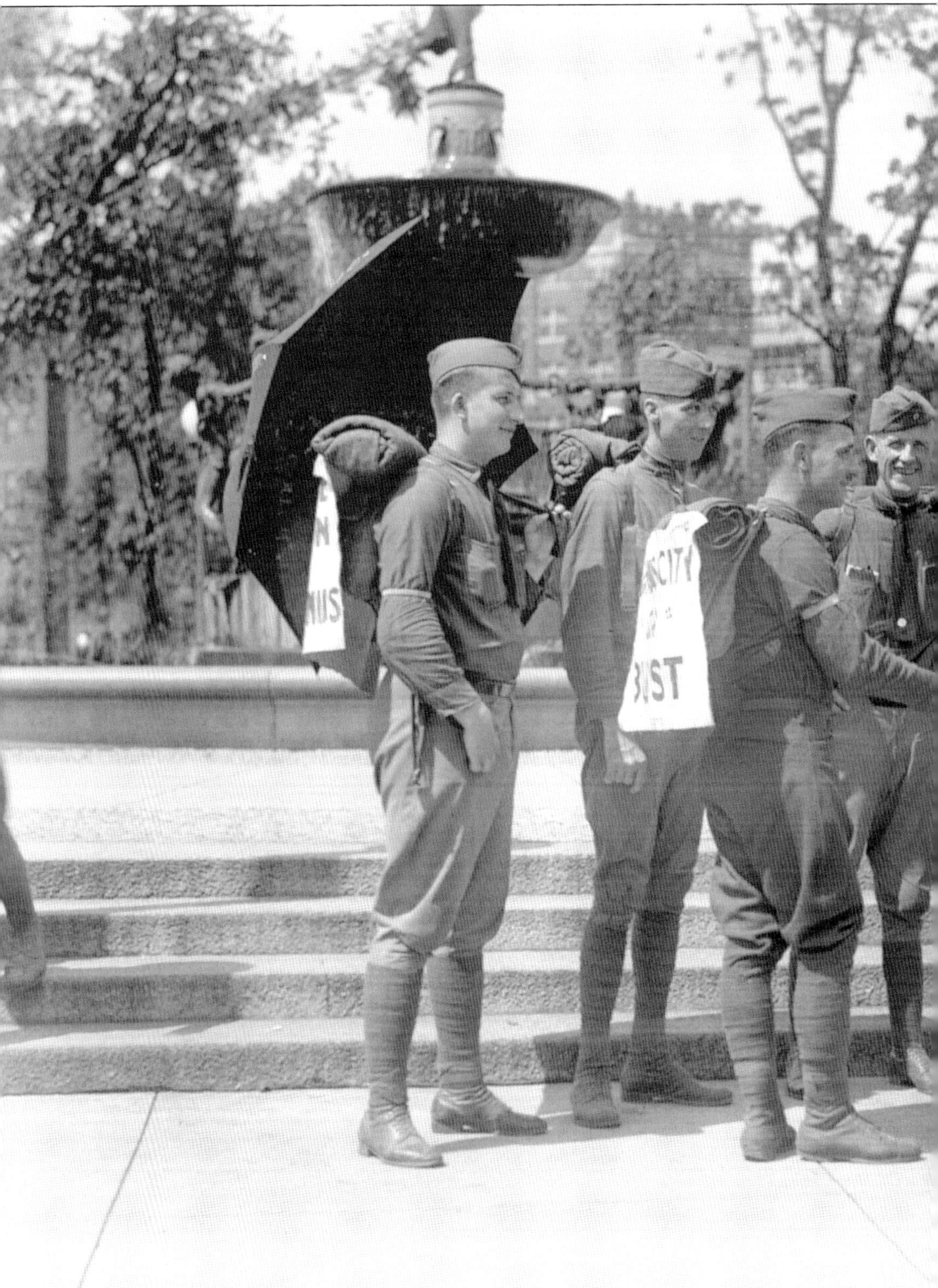
CITY
BUST

A group of former soldiers who served overseas with the American Expeditionary Force visit with a local citizen while in Kansas City for the third national convention of the American Legion in the fall of 1921. During the convention, General Pershing told a crowd of thousands, "If you will accept me as an ordinary buddy in the rear ranks, I will be perfectly contented." (Museum of Missouri Military History.)

Veterans who served with the American Expeditionary Forces in Europe pass by the reviewing stand in front of the Kansas City Star Building during the American Legion Parade on November 1, 1921. The parade was part of the third national convention of the recently formed American Legion and coincided with activities for the dedication of the site for the new Liberty Memorial.

Edgar Cole of Tipton was employed as a locomotive engineer for the Missouri Pacific Railroad and only recently married when he was drafted into the US Army during World War I. Following his training at Camp MacArthur, Texas, Private Cole deployed to France but died from pneumonia on November 13, 1918, two days following the armistice. (Edgar Cole Post 304, American Legion.)

Cole's remains were returned to his wife and mother in Tipton, and he was laid to rest in the community's Masonic Cemetery. According to the 1980 edition of *Moniteau County, Missouri History*, the Edgar Cole Post 304 of the American Legion was first organized around 1921 in honor of Cole's sacrifice in World War I. (Edgar Cole Post 304, American Legion.)

Born in Cape Girardeau on August 11, 1890, Louis K. Juden was a farmer when he entered the Second Officer's Training Camp at Fort Sheridan, Illinois. Following his commissioning, Juden deployed to France in December 1917 and served with the 307th Infantry Regiment and then the 120th Infantry Regiment. During the Meuse-Argonne Offensive, Lieutenant Juden suffered a gas attack and died in a hospital from the effects of gas poisoning on October 26, 1918. The 28-year-old veteran was laid to rest in France; however, since 1919, his legacy has lived on through the Louis K. Juden American Legion Post 63 in Cape Girardeau. (American Legion Post 63.)

Pvt. Wade A Boots from Palmyra enlisted in the United States Marine Corps on February 6, 1918, while attending agriculture classes at the University of Missouri–Columbia. While serving with Company F, 5th Regiment, the Marine was wounded in action in France on November 2, 1918, and died two days later. Although he was initially laid to rest in an American military cemetery overseas, Boots's remains were returned to the United States and reinterred in Greenwood Cemetery in Palmyra. (Courtesy of Boots-Dickson Post 174.)

The Boots-Dickson American Legion Post 174 was established in Palmyra in 1919 and co-named in honor of Pvt. Wade A. Boots and Charles Howard Dickson. According to the November 6, 1935, edition of the *Marion County Standard* of Palmyra, Missouri, Dickson was the second Marion County resident "to be called to the colors under the selective system." Dickson was killed in action on November 1, 1918, while serving with Company D, 354th Infantry and is laid to rest in the Meuse-Argonne American Cemetery in France. (Dwayne Goodwin.)

Twin brothers Roscoe (left) and Robert Enloe were members of Company L, 2nd Missouri Infantry Regiment of Jefferson City when it mobilized for service in World War I and became Company C, 130th Machine Gun Battalion. The 23-year-old Roscoe died on September 30, 1918, from wounds received during the Meuse-Argonne Offensive. The Roscoe Enloe American Legion Post 5 in Jefferson City was chartered in 1919 in honor of his sacrifice.

Following his death, Private Enloe was laid to rest in the Meuse-Argonne American Cemetery in France. Permanent US military cemeteries such as this are administered by an independent agency of the government known as the American Battle Monuments Commission, whose first chairman was former commander of the American Expeditionary Force and Missouri native John J. Pershing.

During World War I, an 18-year-old John W. Jobe of California, Missouri, was serving in the US Army's Company I, 308th when he was killed in action on September 5, 1918. His body was returned to the United States and laid to rest in Crown Hill Cemetery in his hometown. The Jobe-Elliott American Legion Post 17 in California is co-named in his honor. (Moniteau County Historical Society.)

Founded in 1919, the American Legion Auxiliary quickly grew to become the world's largest women's patriotic service organization. Since its inception, the auxiliary has administered scores of programs in support of veterans and volunteered countless hours in its posts and communities. In 1931, the American Legion Auxiliary dedicated this plaque in the east wing of the Missouri Capitol as a memorial to the men and women of the state who served in World War I.

Pvt. Emilio Rollo was assigned to the 101st Infantry Regiment of the 26th Division when he was killed in action on October 23, 1918. A native of Italy, Rollo's family later immigrated to "The Hill"—the Italian section of St. Louis. According to his draft registration card, he was married and employed as a sewer worker with the City of St. Louis when he was inducted into the US Army on October 3, 1917. Following his death, the soldier was interred in the Meuse-Argonne American Cemetery in France. (Rollo-Calcaterra American Legion Post 15.)

Rollo-Calcaterra American Legion Post 15 was chartered on May 14, 1946, and is located in the historical Italian section of St. Louis known as The Hill. The post is co-named in honor of the late Emilio Rollo, an Italian immigrant killed during the Meuse-Argonne Offensive, and M.Sgt. Angelo E. Calcaterra, who was killed while serving with the US Army Air Forces in World War II. (Rollo-Calcaterra American Legion Post 15.)

After World War I, the Gold Star Mothers of St. Louis created a memorial consisting of 1,185 bronze plaques with the names of local veterans killed in the war. The memorial was once part of the boulevard of Kings Highway but was removed in the 1980s when the highway was widened. The Rollo-Calcaterra American Legion Post 15 helped rescue 752 of the bronze plaques and spearheaded a project to develop the World War I Court of Honor Memorial at Jefferson Barracks National Cemetery, which contains the majority of the plaques. The plaque for one of the post's namesakes, Emilio Rollo, is displayed on a marker in front of the post's St. Louis home. (Rollo-Calcaterra American Legion Post 15.)

This vintage postcard shows a decorative drinking fountain installed by the American Legion in 1921 at the intersection of Ninth and Main Streets in Kansas City. The fountain was relocated in the late 1950s to the Budd Park Esplanade at Van Brunt Boulevard and Anderson Avenue. The shaft of the fountain has two brass panels—one features soldiers and the other shows sailors engaged in combat activities in World War I.

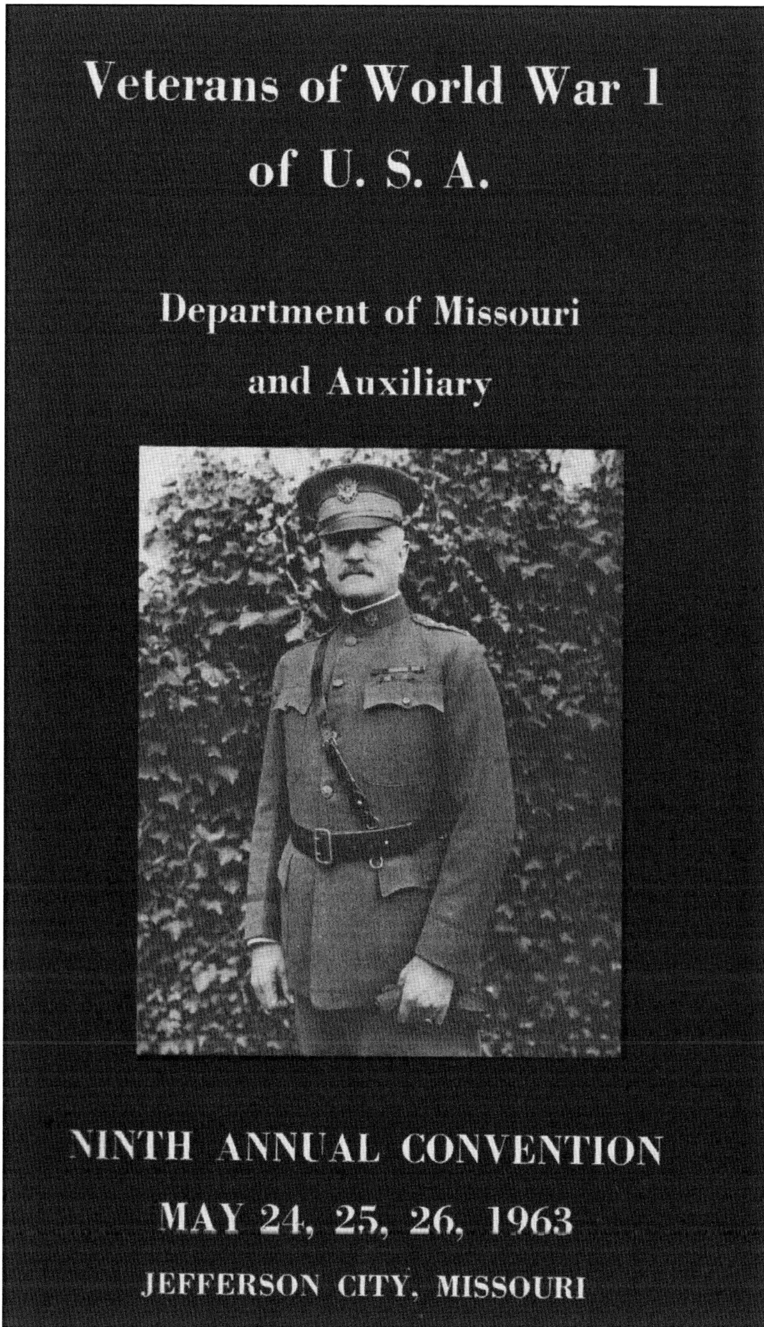

The Veterans of World War I of USA. Inc. (VWWI) was incorporated by Congress on July 18, 1958, and supported those who served honorably in the armed forces during World War I, providing aid to their surviving families and dependents in addition to advocating for legislation and laws. Like many service organizations, the VWWI adopted a constitution and bylaws and was structured on a national basis with subdivisions of departments, districts, and barracks, the latter of which referred to local chapters. This booklet was given to members of the organization attending the VWWI Department of Missouri annual convention in Jefferson City in 1963.

Eligibility for membership in the VWWI began with the United States' declaration of war on April 6, 1917, and ended on Armistice Day, November 11, 1918. Eligibility was extended to veterans who served in Siberia from November 11, 1918, to July 1, 1921, as part of the American Expeditionary Force, Siberia. Missouri was home to many local posts, known as barracks, such as Barracks No. 221 in Kansas City, whose number is stitched on this service cap worn by a former member. In 2010, there was only one remaining member of the organization, Missouri native Frank Buckles, who passed the following year.

Similar in structure to organizations such as the Veterans of Foreign Wars and the American Legion, the VWWI had an auxiliary membership program for spouses of World War I veterans. This service cap belonged to a member of VWWI Barracks 1191 in Poplar Bluff, Missouri, and features the patch of the VWWI Auxiliary. In later years, one of the primary objectives of the VWWI was to encourage legislation that would expand the pension program available to veterans of the First World War. In 1963, the VWWI ranked as the third-largest veterans organization in the country.

In November 1941, a majority of the past commanders from American Legion Post 5 in Jefferson City gathered for this photograph. The group of World War I veterans included Ed Arnett (top row, far left, next to flag), who became commander in 1942 and served alongside the post's namesake, Pvt. Roscoe Enloe, in Company C, 130th Machine Gun Battalion during the war. (American Legion Post 5.)

Seven

Legacies and Memorials

An unprecedented gathering of military heroes of the world war occurred in Kansas City in 1921, when thousands assembled for the national convention of the American Legion. It was the first time the primary military leaders of the war all assembled in one place. Pictured are, from left to right, Lt. Gen. Baron Jacques of Belgium, Gen. Armando Diaz of Italy, Pres. Calvin Coolidge, Gen. Ferdinand Foch of France, unidentified, Adm. David Beatty of England, and Gen. John J. Pershing.

Queen Marie of Romania visited Kansas City in 1926 during an extended tour of the United States. While there, she attended the dedication of the new Liberty Memorial and laid a wreath to honor those killed in the war. Queen Marie became quite popular because of her personal involvement with citizens, and despite her fame and notoriety during World War I, she volunteered to serve as a nurse with the Red Cross.

The Liberty Memorial Association was officially formed at the Hotel Muehlebach (pictured on this vintage postcard) in Kansas City on December 20, 1918. The group's purpose was the construction of a grand monument in Kansas City to serve as a memorial for those who gave their lives in World War I. The property selected for the memorial was the hillside on the south side of Kansas City's Union Station so that it would be seen by those traveling through the area.

Thousands of citizens gathered on the south side of Union Station in Kansas City for the dedication of the site for the Liberty Memorial on November 1, 1921. During the dedication, Robert A. Long, president of the Liberty Memorial Association, prepared a message of peace that was delivered to Pres. Warren Harding by carrier pigeon. The message read, in part, "Peace must become the creed of the world; disarmament must become the code of the nations."

The American Legion parade held in Kansas City during the dedication of the site of the Liberty Memorial in 1921 grew into such a significant event that the US Postal Service suspended service on the day of the parade so that letter carriers in the area would be able to attend the historic event.

The dedication for the Liberty Memorial was held on November 11, 1926, during a ceremony attended by Pres. Calvin Coolidge. The newly constructed memorial site featured two exhibit halls—Memory Hall, located on the east side of the Liberty Memorial Tower, and Exhibit Hall, located on the west side of the tower. From 1926 to 2004, Exhibit Hall served as the primary gallery space for the Liberty Memorial.

This linen postcard shows the Liberty Memorial in Kansas City as it appeared in the 1930s. Construction on the 217-foot-tall memorial began in 1923 with four guardian spirits adorning the top section of the tower and two Assyrian sphinxes on either side of the base. The flame that appears to emanate from the crest of the tower is achieved through a steam and light display.

Every Negro should do his or her part in the Great Campaign for

The Liberty War Memorial

Local Allied Charities

October 27th to November 1st

Remember the Negro boys who died for your liberty. They will have a place in this Memorial.

Remember the needy—our own Charities. They will share in this. The payments are easy.

NEGRO CAMPAIGN HEADQUARTERS
Y. M. C. A. BUILDING
DR. T. C. UNTHANK, Chairman

To raise funds for the construction of the Liberty Memorial, the association sponsored a public fundraising drive in the fall of 1919. A goal of $2.5 million was established, with $2 million slated for the construction of the Liberty Memorial and another $500,000 for Allied charities. On November 6, 1919, it was announced that the fundraising goal had been achieved, with contributions totaling $2.517 million. African American citizens were also called upon to support the drive to ensure their sacrifices in the war were not forgotten, as noted in this solicitation appearing in the *Kansas City Sun* newspaper.

The Liberty Memorial was closed in 1994 because of safety concerns related to deterioration. Restoration was achieved through private donations and funds received from the city, state, and federal governments. In 2004, it was designated by Congress as the nation's official World War I museum and construction began on a new 80,000-square-foot research center and museum under the memorial. The memorial was designated a national historic landmark in 2006 and reopened to the public the same year.

A wooden memorial arch was erected in downtown Jefferson City for a homecoming parade held on October 7, 1919, honoring Cole County's fallen heroes. The parade began at the state capitol and proceeded down High Street, coming to an end at McClung Park. The community held a barbecue that included several forms of entertainment for local service members and their families. Newspapers reported that an estimated 20,000 people showed up for the day's activities. According to census records, the population of the county in 1920 was 24,680. (VFW Post 1003.)

A victory celebration was held in St. Charles on September 1, 1919, to celebrate the return of local service members. The event opened with a homecoming parade comprised of thousands of uniformed servicemen as well as two women who had served overseas; the war-wounded rode in automobiles during the parade. The event ended in Blanchette Park, where the service members were assembled and then dismissed to enjoy the day's activities that included dinner and dancing.

The Call of Missouri is a painting by famed muralist Edwin Blashfield; it was commissioned by the Kansas City chapter of the Daughters of the American Revolution in 1918. The painting mysteriously disappeared from its original home in the early 1980s and has since been sold at auction and purchased by an unknown collector.

The Missouri legislature appropriated $25,000 on May 5, 1919, for the purpose of constructing a memorial to commemorate the heroism of Missourians who served in France during World War I. Nancy Coonsman Hahn of St. Louis was selected to create the monument on a site near Cheppy, France, near where a St. Louis veteran, Capt. Alexander Skinker, was killed in action and was subsequently awarded the Medal of Honor.

Missouri became the first state to erect a memorial in France to honor her sons who perished in the war. The memorial was named "Victory" and was dedicated during a ceremony held on November 5, 1922, and presided over by Field Marshall Joseph Joffre—commander in chief of French forces early in World War I. The design of the memorial features a bronze figure situated on top of a granite base, which is a woman looking toward the sky grasping a victory wreath of laurel in her raised right hand while holding an olive branch in her other hand. The base of the memorial is emblazoned with the state seal of Missouri. (Museum of Missouri Military History.)

Below the state seal on the base of the Missouri World War I memorial in France is an inscription in both English and French, which reads, "Erected by the State of Missouri, United States of America, to the memory of her sons who died in France for humanity during the Great War 1917–1918." The memorial is on a triangular piece of land approximately a half-mile from Cheppy, a location associated with engagements of the 35th and 89th Divisions, both of which were heavily populated with Missouri soldiers in World War I. (Museum of Missouri Military History.)

Following the dedication of Missouri's World War I memorial in France in 1922, appropriations by the Missouri General Assembly for its upkeep were overlooked and the monument fell into disrepair. The 71st General Assembly appropriated $15,000 for repairs, and the 72nd General Assembly reappropriated those funds and added an additional $2,500. The repair work, through contract assistance provided by the American Battle Monuments Commission, was completed in the summer of 1964. (Museum of Missouri Military History.)

The Missouri General Assembly has continued to monitor the condition of Missouri's World War I memorial in France and appropriates funds in an effort to maintain its integrity and appearance. In 1983, a $12,000 appropriation was made to re-bronze the statue and perform repair work on the granite pedestal and the steps leading to the memorial. (Museum of Missouri Military History.)

The Clay County World War I doughboy statue, which cost the community $3,000 and stands outside of the Clay County Courthouse in Liberty, was dedicated in May 1921 in honor of local men who served during the war. During the three draft registrations that occurred during the war, an estimated 4,341 Clay County men registered for military service as part of the Selective Service Act of 1917.

With a cost of $250,000 to construct, Memorial Hall in Joplin was dedicated in honor of area veterans, both living and dead, on October 18, 1925, before an estimated crowd of 2,000 people. The principal speaker at the dedication ceremony was World War I veteran Col. E.M. Stayton, who was at the time serving as the state commander of the American Legion.

Carthage Memorial Hall was dedicated on September 12, 1924. Built to honor local service members killed in World War I, the auditorium and meeting rooms are now used for local events such as concerts, wedding receptions, and corporate meetings. The second floor is utilized by the American Legion Edwin Wiggins Post 9, which was named for a Carthage soldier killed in action during the Meuse-Argonne Offensive while serving with a federalized Missouri National Guard company.

Shortly after the end of World War I, the Missouri General Assembly requested that the superintendent of schools for each county lead a fundraising campaign to produce a banner to present to the state and to be hung in the state capitol. The banner for Pemiscot County, pictured here, was created by Llewellyn Barry Phillips, a war widow from Caruthersville, Missouri. Her husband, Lt. Pierre S. Phillips, died from pneumonia on October 22, 1918, while overseas with the US Army. (Missouri State Museum, Missouri State Parks.)

Sixty-six counties presented their banners to the Missouri adjutant general in April 1919. Throughout the next two decades, an additional 26 county banners were donated to the state. Included in this collection is the banner for Harrison County in northwest Missouri. This banner includes four red crosses, which is believed to represent four county residents who served with the American Red Cross during World War I. (Missouri State Museum, Missouri State Parks.)

The 92 county service banners remain in the collection of the Missouri State Museum. The banner presented by McDonald County in southwest Missouri shows that 444 county residents served in the military during World War I, while the gold stars denote 24 who lost their lives in the service. On the sides of the banner are vertical ribbons that list the names of all from the county who served, while the horizontal white ribbon at the top lists the names of those killed in the war. (Missouri State Museum, Missouri State Parks.)

Plans for the construction of a student union began in 1915 at the University of Missouri–Columbia; however, World War I delayed its construction. The building was completed in 1926 and named Memorial Tower in honor of the university students who died during the war. The initial cost for the construction of the tower was $288,000.

Initially, Memorial Tower consisted of a bell tower, which is pictured in this vintage postcard. Years later, additional phases of construction added a north wing, the A.P. Green Chapel, and a south wing. The ceiling of the archway of Memorial Tower is inscribed with the names of the 117 university students who died in the war along with a plaque reminding those passing through to tip their hats as a sign of respect to those whose names are listed above.

This Eternal Flame located near the Soldiers Memorial Military Museum in downtown St. Louis was erected in 1935 by the Monuments Builders of America in recognition of the founding of the American Legion. The American Legion was established during a meeting of World War I veterans between May 8 and 10, 1918, at the former Schubert Theater in St. Louis. The monument consists of a tall granite column that supports a copper stand with an eternal flame.

Rulif Martin was in college when he was inducted into the Missouri National Guard in July 1917. He deployed to France in May 1918, serving with a machine-gun battalion. After the war, he married and became an advertising agent but soon displayed symptoms of "shell shock," now known as post-traumatic stress disorder. His wife reported him missing in early 1922 and later discovered he suffered from memory loss. Martin was found three months later working for a newspaper in Colorado and was reunited with his family, went on to raise two daughters, and was employed as a newspaper editor in Rolla for many years. (Museum of Missouri Military History.)

Communities often sought to recognize local veterans who served in the war by minting and presenting special medals, such as this one bestowed by the people of St. Louis to soldiers of the 12th Engineers (Light Railway.) The 12th Engineers was organized in St. Louis in the late spring and early summer of 1917 and went on to perform critical railway work in Europe during World War I. It was one of the first regiments to land overseas and is believed to be the first American unit to receive enemy fire in the war.

The community of Mountain Grove joined many others throughout the country that chose to honor their local veterans of World War I with a monument in town square. Like many such memorials in the state, it was funded in part by the County Memorial Act passed by the Missouri General Assembly in 1919.

The Saline County World War I memorial is pictured outside the county courthouse in Marshall during a World War I centennial event held in September 2018. The memorial was first unveiled on October 12, 1927, and was named "Over the Top" by designer and American sculptor John Paulding.

The American Legion Post 16 dedicated a monument to local veterans killed in World War I on the lawn of the Pettis County Courthouse in Sedalia on November 12, 1926. The dedication was delayed by one day so that local residents could travel to Kansas City on Armistice Day (now Veterans Day) to attend the dedication of the Liberty Memorial, where Pres. Calvin Coolidge was in attendance. The base of the Pettis County monument was later updated with the names of local casualties of World War II, Korea, and Vietnam.

This real-photo postcard features the World War I memorial that was erected on the campus of the former Wentworth Military Academy in Lexington. Unveiled in a ceremony on June 10, 1923, the statue is the E.M. Viquensney–designed *The Spirit of the American Doughboy* and features an American infantry soldier dressed in an olive drab uniform with wrapped leggings and a steel helmet. According to a history of Wentworth published in 1950, the statue honors the more than 500 students who served in World War I, 16 of whom were killed and 19 of whom were wounded in action.

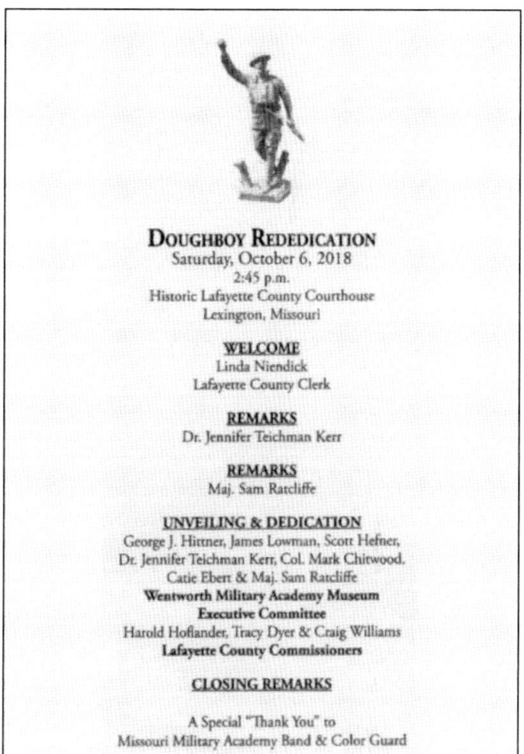

DOUGHBOY REDEDICATION
Saturday, October 6, 2018
2:45 p.m.
Historic Lafayette County Courthouse
Lexington, Missouri

WELCOME
Linda Niendick
Lafayette County Clerk

REMARKS
Dr. Jennifer Teichman Kerr

REMARKS
Maj. Sam Ratcliffe

UNVEILING & DEDICATION
George J. Hittner, James Lowman, Scott Hefner,
Dr. Jennifer Teichman Kerr, Col. Mark Chitwood,
Catie Ebert & Maj. Sam Ratcliffe
Wentworth Military Academy Museum
Executive Committee
Harold Hoflander, Tracy Dyer & Craig Williams
Lafayette County Commissioners

CLOSING REMARKS

A Special "Thank You" to
Missouri Military Academy Band & Color Guard

The historic Wentworth Military Academy closed its doors in 2017 due to financial difficulties after 137 years of educating students and cadets. The Wentworth Military Academy Alumni Association was able to acquire possession of the World War I statue, and during a ceremony held on October 6, 2018, it was rededicated at a new location on the lawn of the Lafayette County Courthouse in Lexington.

The Missouri General Assembly authorized on April 23, 1919, a medal for state residents who served in the National Guard or the US armed forces during World War I. According to the Missouri National Guard, the medals were bronze and made by the D.L. Auld Company at a cost of approximately 25¢ each.

Pictured is the reverse side of the Missouri World War I medal. To qualify, a state resident must have served in a qualifying military status on active duty during the period of April 6, 1917, through November 11, 1918, if a member of the US armed forces, or between August 5, 1917, through November 11, 1918, if a member of the National Guard.

Pvt. James Roy Sone was a US Marine from Jefferson City who was killed in action while serving in France on October 4, 1918. He was initially laid to rest in France, but his body was returned to the states and interred in Jefferson City in 1921. This painting of the World War I veteran was unveiled during a ceremony held at the state capitol in 1924. It now hangs in the clubroom of VFW Post 1003 in St. Martins near Jefferson City.

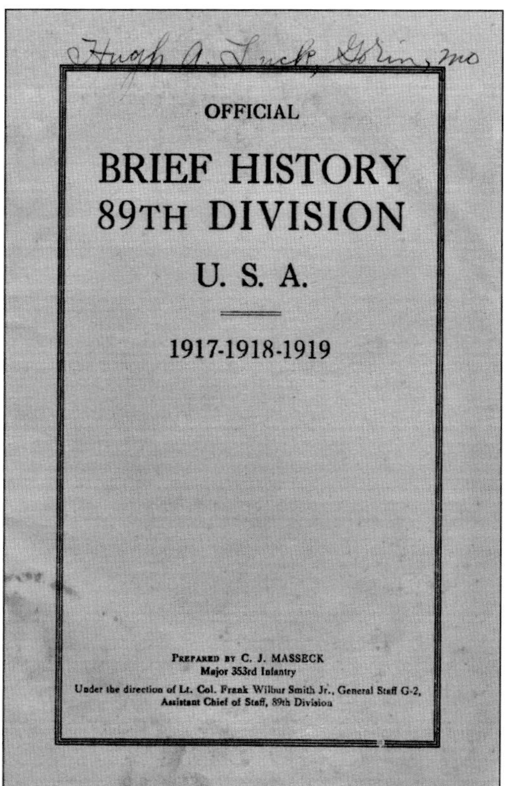

Hugh A. Luck, Gorin, Mo

OFFICIAL

BRIEF HISTORY
89TH DIVISION

U. S. A.

1917-1918-1919

PREPARED BY C. J. MASSECK
Major 353rd Infantry
Under the direction of Lt. Col. Frank Wilbur Smith Jr., General Staff G-2,
Assistant Chief of Staff, 89th Division

This 48-page booklet belonging to Hugh A. Luck was published shortly after the end of World War I and provided highlights regarding the wartime service of soldiers of the 89th Infantry Division. Luck, who was from Gorin, Missouri, rose to the rank of sergeant while assigned to Company A, 354th Infantry. He served overseas from June 4, 1918, to May 22, 1919. The veteran lived to be 94 years old, passing away on July 26, 1988. He is buried in Harmony Grove Cemetery in Knox County, Missouri.

Inside the dim interior of the Pershing Gallery in the Missouri State Capitol in Jefferson City is this large painting dedicated to the service of Gen. John J. Pershing in World War I. The detailed painting shows Pershing rendering a salute to the Marquis de Lafayette when visiting the tomb of the famed French military commander at Picpus Cemetery in Paris on July 4, 1917. It was during this visit that Lt. Col. Charles E. Stanton made a speech on behalf of Pershing during which he coined the phrase, "Lafayette, we are here!"

This bronze statue of General Pershing, commander of the American Expeditionary Force in World War I, was erected in 1957, four years after the general assembly appropriated $25,000 for its creation. It was initially placed on the east grounds of the Missouri State Capitol, but in 1968, it was moved to the General John J. Pershing Boyhood Home State Historic Site in Laclede.

General Pershing made his final public appearance at the Armistice Day ceremonies held in Arlington National Cemetery on November 11, 1942. The 87-year-old Missouri native died of congestive heart failure at Walter Reed Medical Center on July 15, 1948. He was laid to rest in Arlington National Cemetery. Nearly 63 years later, the last American World War I veteran—and fellow Missourian—Frank Buckles, was also laid to rest in Arlington.

Following the armistice, General Pershing submitted his report to the secretary of war, dated November 20, 1918. The report served as a summary of the organization and operations of the American Expeditionary Force throughout the war. Herzig and McLean of New York published the report as a booklet in 1919 under the title *General Pershing's Story of the American Army in France.*

On November 11, 1921, in the House of Representatives chamber at the Missouri State Capitol, Gov. Arthur M. Hyde signed the Soldier's Bonus Bill and presented it to soldiers of Missouri. Accepting the bill were Ed Arnett, a Missouri National Guardsman who served in World War I, along with several of his fellow veterans who two years earlier helped establish American Legion Post 5 in Jefferson City. Governor Hyde went on to become the secretary of agriculture under Pres. Herbert Hoover in 1929. (American Legion Post 5.)

Bibliography

Amick, Jeremy P. *Soldierly Devotion: World War I through the Eyes of a Missouri Farmer.* Harrisonville, MO: Burnt District Press LLC, 2015.

Browe, Amanda. *From the Archives: Women of the Canteen Service.* American Red Cross. March 6, 2014.

History of the Missouri National Guard. Published by the Authority of the Military Council, Missouri National Guard: November 1934.

Lee, Van. *Vin Rouge, Vin Blanc, Beaucoup Vin, the American Expeditionary Force in WWI.* Hattiesburg, MS: Realms of Mertox Productions, 2004.

"Legion Magazines Heading to Digital Archive." *The American Legion.* June 12, 2014.

"Memorial to War Heroes Dedicated at Kansas City." *St. Louis Star and Times.* November 1, 1921: 2.

Newman, John J. *Uncle, We Are Ready!* North Salt Lake, UT: Heritage Quest, 2001.

"Send Men to Officers Training Camp." *Mexico Weekly Ledger.* June 11, 1918: 2.

Settle, Raymond W. *The Story of Wentworth.* Kansas City, MO: Spencer Printing Company, 1950.

Consistent with our mission to preserve history on a local level, this book was printed in South Carolina on American-made paper and manufactured entirely in the United States. Products carrying the accredited Forest Stewardship Council (FSC) label are printed on 100 percent FSC-certified paper.

MADE IN THE USA